Ask & it Shall be Given: Three Steps to Guaranteed Results in Prayer

By Benjamin L. Reynolds

Discover other titles by this author at
http://www.benjaminlreynolds.com and discover other
titles at **http://amazon.com/author/benjaminreynolds**

ISBN-13: 978-1482503975
ISBN-10: 1482503972

Printed in the United States of America
Copyright © 2013 by Benjamin L. Reynolds

D0107474

248
Rey

Table of Contents

INTRODUCTION 4

PART 1 - ASKING 6

    LEARNING HOW TO ASK 7

PART 2 – SEEKING GOD 53

    SEEKING GOD IS A JOURNEY OF DISCOVERY 54

PREPARING FOR THE JOURNEY 70

PART 3 - KNOCKING 96

    OVERCOMING OBSTACLES 97

PART 4 - 7 DAY DEVOTIONAL 109

DEVOTIONAL PART 1 110

    DAY 1 - MORNING DEVOTION 111

    DAY 1 - EVENING DEVOTION 114

    DAY 2 - MORNING DEVOTION 117

    DAY 2 - EVENING DEVOTION 120

    DAY 3 - MORNING DEVOTION 123

    DAY 3 - EVENING·DEVOTION 126

DEVOTIONAL PART 2 129

    DAY 4 - MORNING DEVOTION 130

    DAY 4 - EVENING DEVOTION 134

    DAY 5 - MORNING DEVOTION 137

    DAY 5 - EVENING DEVOTION 140

DEVOTIONAL PART 3 143

    DAY 6 - MORNING DEVOTION 144

DAY 6 - EVENING DEVOTION 147

DAY 7 - MORNING DEVOTION 150

DAY 7 - EVENING DEVOTION 153

AUTHOR BIOGRAPHY 156

MORE FROM BENJAMIN L. REYNOLDS 158

INTRODUCTION

"Ask, and it will be given to you; seek, and you will find; knock, and it will be opened to you. For everyone who asks receives, and the one who seeks finds, and to the one who knocks it will be opened." Matthew 7:7-8 ESV

Jesus made three specific promises about prayer:

1. Everyone *asking* in prayer would receive.

2. Everyone *seeking* in prayer would find.

3. Everyone *knocking* on spiritual doors in prayer would have them opened.

These are 100% guarantees. With such incredible guarantees, why are we not receiving everything we pray for? If Matthew 7:7-8 were true, prayer should be as simple as asking and receiving every time. For some reason, it's not, *but it can be.* If we want to receive guaranteed answers to our prayers, we need to examine what it means to *Ask, Seek and Knock. Asking* may seem as simple as looking toward heave and saying a few words, but what about *Seeking* and *Knocking?* With a 100% guarantee of getting what we ask for, isn't it worth the effort to find out what *Asking, Seeking and Knocking* really mean?

This book is divided into three sections that examine *Asking, Seeking and Knocking*, followed by a 7 day devotional. I recommend reading the first three sections of the book before starting the devotional to get a solid understanding of what *Asking, Seeking and Knocking* really mean. Also, before starting the devotion, determine what you want to ask God for and set time aside each day (morning and evening) for study and prayer. Try to be consistent with your prayer and study time.

God Bless and May the Lord keep you on the journey you are about to begin.

PART 1 - ASKING

LEARNING HOW TO ASK

You are probably thinking, "Isn't asking simply saying Lord I need this" or "Lord I need that?" Well, not exactly. If asking were that simple, every praying would have everything they needed. Asking God for something requires more than simply saying, "Hey God, can you please bless me with this or that." Sure, there are times when we can rattle off a few words in prayer and receive a response, but if we want to become more effective in prayer and receive 100% of what we pray for, then we must learn the proper way to ask. For example, let us say you need one hundred thousand dollars and go to the bank and ask for a loan. How would you ask for the money? Would you begin by screaming or crying, demanding that someone give you money? Would you approach a teller and beg for money? Probably not. Ideally, you would locate a loan officer, who would ask you a series of questions, and then present you with an application. In the application, you would list who you are, what you do, and the purpose of the loan. This would be the proper way to ask for a large sum of money. Similarly, there is a proper way to ask God to supply the things you need in prayer.

Asking for help is not easy. We often think asking for help carries a negative connotation, signifies weakness, or means we are somehow inadequate. If we want to get better results in prayer and see the rich blessings of God, that negative mindset must disappear. There will always be times when we need help from people and even more times when we need help from God. The greatest men and women in the Bible needed God's during their lives and we are no different. Since there will be many times when no one can help us but God, we might as well get good at asking.

Fortunately, the Bible is rich in examples of how to ask God for what we need in prayer. The best example is in Matthew 6:5-15, where Jesus gives his disciples instructions on how to pray.

(5) And when you pray, you must not be like the hypocrites. For they love to stand and pray in the synagogues and at the street corners, that they may be seen by others. Truly, I say to you, they have received their reward.

(6) But when you pray, go into your room and shut the door and pray to your Father who is in secret. And your Father who sees in secret will reward you.

Interpretation: Jesus is telling his disciples not to be hypocritical in prayer, doing things publicly to receive attention and rewards from others, but not from God. Instead, the majority of our prayers should consist of private, intimate conversations with God. These conversations will garner God's attention and rewards.

(7) And when you pray, do not heap up empty phrases as the Gentiles do, for they

think that they will be heard for their many words.

Interpretation: Pray with sincere, heartfelt emotion instead of repeating scripted prayers. God prefers real conversation with us, not recitation, and repetition. Imagine having a conversation with someone where one or both people only repeat scripted phrases. How boring and unrealistic would that be? How do you think God feels when we use scripted prayers and recitations instead of real conversation? Talk to God honestly and sincerely and will do the same with you.

(8) Do not be like them, for your Father knows what you need before you ask him.

Interpretation: God knows what we are going to pray about before we pray. For him, it is about quality, not quantity in prayer. God wants sincerity and devotion, not meaningless words and time spent praying.

(9) Pray then like this: "Our Father in heaven, hallowed be your name.

Interpretation: This is how you do it the right way. Glorify God for who he is, what he has done.

(10) Your kingdom come, your will be done, on earth as it is in heaven.

Interpretation: Glorify God for what you want him to do for you in the future. Pray for the kingdom of God to be established in the Earth and his will to be done in your life and in the lives of others like it is in heaven.

(11) Give us this day our daily bread,

Interpretation: Ask God for help with the things you need each day.

(12) And forgive us our debts, as we also have forgiven our debtors.

Interpretation: Ask God to forgive your sins and be sure to forgive anyone who has offended or hurt you. Forgiveness is the most important part of the Lord's Prayer and Jesus stresses the necessity of forgiving others Matthew 6:14-15. I believe Jesus emphasized this portion of the prayer because it is easily overlooked and the most difficult to do. We want forgiveness from God and others, but are often unwilling to forgive those who we feel have wronged us. True forgiveness requires that we give it to receive it.

(13) And lead us not into temptation, but deliver us from evil.

Interpretation: Ask God to keep you from situations, people, places, and things that may affect your walk with Christ. Avoiding sin and temptation is easier than trying to resist amid sin. Pray for God to deliver you from trying circumstances that exist in your life or those you may encounter. Overcoming evil is far easier when we ask God for help.

What Jesus taught about the Lord's Prayer can be divided into two parts. The first part is Matthew 6:5-8, where Jesus teaches the disciples what attitude they should have in prayer. The second part is Matthew 6:9-15, where Jesus teaches what important topics we should discuss in prayer. In Matthew 6:5-8, Jesus teaches two things about our attitude when praying:

1. Do not be hypocritical in prayer, wanting only to be seen and heard by others. Instead, find a private place to talk with God.

2. Do not use meaningless, repetitious words in prayer. Instead, pray from the heart about what you really need since God already knows your needs anyway.

In Matthew 6:9-15, the second part of the prayer, there are seven things Jesus tells his disciples to discuss in prayer:

1. Praise and make the Lord's name holy.
2. Pray for God's kingdom to be established.
3. Pray for God's will to be done in our lives.
4. Pray for God to give you what you need to get through the day.
5. Ask for forgiveness and forgive the sins of others.
6. Ask to be kept from temptation.
7. Ask to be delivered from evil.

The nine items Jesus tells his disciples to use in prayer shows that asking means a lot more than saying, "Please give me" or "can I please have this?" Asking for something in prayer is similar to my previous example of asking for a loan. For example, if someone wants to increase the odds of qualifying for a bank loan, they will fill out the bank's application, following all instructions and supplying any necessary information. Likewise, if we want to guarantee our odds of receiving what we ask for in prayer, we need to follow all of God's instructions.

To help incorporate The Lord's Prayer into my prayer life, I created and used a Lord's Prayer Guide. In the guide, I separate the seven distinct subjects Jesus tells his disciples to pray about in Matthew 6:9-13. I then associated related reference scriptures with each topic, and then incorporated them into my prayer routine. While most people recite the entire Lord's prayer at once, I find it more enriching to focus on each subject, praying the scriptures or relating personal experience, and then moving on to the next subject. A copy of the guide I created is available for free on my website.

THE MOMENT WE ASK IN PRAYER, THE PROCESS OF BLESSING BEGINS

"In those days I, Daniel, was mourning for three weeks. I ate no delicacies, no meat or wine entered my mouth, nor did I anoint myself at all, for the full three weeks. On the twenty-fourth day of the first month, as I was standing on the bank of the great

river (that is, the Tigris) I lifted up my eyes and looked, and behold, a man clothed in linen, with a belt of fine gold from Uphaz around his waist."
Daniel 10:2-5 ESV

"Then he said to me, "Fear not, Daniel, for from the first day that you set your heart to understand and humbled yourself before your God, your words have been heard, and I have come because of your words."
Daniel 10:12 ESV

The prophet Daniel practiced *Asking, Seeking, and Knocking*. After three weeks of praying, fasting, and seeking God, the angel Gabriel appeared to him with an answer. Gabriel did not just give Daniel the answer to his prayer; he let him know that God heard the prayer the first day that it was made! Sometimes we get discouraged after many days, weeks, months, or years of praying when we do not receive and answer. We wonder if God heard us or if we are doing something wrong. The angel Gabriel let Daniel know that God heard his prayer and even told him the reason for the delayed answer:

> *"The prince of the kingdom of Persia withstood me twenty-one days, but Michael, one of the chief princes, came to help me, for I*

was left there with the kings of Persia, and came to make you understand what is to happen to your people in the latter days. For the vision is for days yet to come." Daniel 10:13-14 ESV

Strong, demonic forces fought against Gabriel to prevent him from delivering God's response to Daniel's prayer. So important was the prophetic answer that Satan commanded the demonic leader overseeing the ancient kingdom of Persia to marshal his forces and spend three weeks fighting at all cost to keep Daniel from hearing what he needed. Understand there are many reasons that we do not receive immediate responses to our prayers. Many times, it is because Satan and his demonic host know that if we receive the answers we are praying for, the world may be changed. Satan's forces strive to delay the answers to our prayers so we will become discouraged and doubtful. We must remain patient, steadfast, and encouraged because the longer the delay, the bigger the blessing! Daniel was unaware that his prayer was a threat to Satan's kingdom and a blessing for the kingdom of God until the answer came. We will receive an answer to many things when God finally answers our prayer; including how important we are and what a blessing we are to the kingdom of God. Stay encouraged and keep asking the Lord to answer your prayer because in doing so, you will stay encouraged and encourage others.

WHEN YOU ASK IN PRAYER, DO NOT DOUBT IT WILL BE ANSWERED

"And Jesus answered them, "Truly, I say to you, if you have faith and do not doubt, you will not only do what has been done to the fig tree, but even if you say to this mountain, 'Be taken up and thrown into the sea,' it will happen. And whatever you ask in prayer, you will receive, if you have faith." Matthew 21:21-22 ESV

In Matthew 21:21-22, Jesus tells us that when our faith is 100% of what it should be, we will be able to achieve the impossible. We will be able to move mountains and defy nature as Jesus did by withering the fig tree in Matthew 21:17-20. Doubt removes our ability to receive from God and makes what was once possible, impossible. Jesus tells us that it is pointless to ask for something if you do not believe you will receive it. God requires absolute faith before he begins to answer prayer. Jesus tells us that if we absolutely believe what we are asking for in prayer, then nothing is impossible for us. Did you hear that? God has promised we can receive **WHATEVER** we ask for if we ask with one hundred percent faith. **WHATEVER WE ASK FOR, IF WE HAVE FAITH**. Do you understand what that means? **WHATEVER WE ASK FOR** means anything we dream of. **WHATEVER WE ASK FOR** means never having to worry about bills. **WHATEVER WE ASK FOR** means always having enough to care for our families and ourselves. **WHATEVER WE ASK FOR** means what is says, **WHATEVER WE ASK FOR** can mean a lot . . . and all we need is faith to unlock it. Faith is the key that unlocks **WHATEVER WE ASK FOR**. It turns the ignition switch that starts the process of blessing. A lack of faith is the same as not having a key to start the ignition.

When we pray without faith, the blessing process becomes stalled.

> "But let him ask in faith, with no doubting, for the one who doubts is like a wave of the sea that is driven and tossed by the wind. For that person must not suppose that he will receive anything from the Lord; he is a double-minded man, unstable in all his ways."
> James 1:6-8 ESV

God does not bless people who lack faith for several reasons:

1. When we ask God to do something in our lives and then doubt, it shows that we are double-minded. God will not bless a double-minded, unstable person because he cannot depend on them to express his divine will and glory.
2. A double-minded person is unstable and untrustworthy, making them unfit to represent God and his kingdom. When God chooses to act, he does so out of divine mercy and grace, wanting to receive praise and glory for what he has

done.[1] An unstable, double-minded person cannot be trusted to praise, magnify and make God look as good and glorious as he should be. If you had a business or product, would you choose someone with a bad, untrustworthy image or someone who represents class, quality, and faithfulness? Likewise, if we want God to answer our prayers, we must show faith in him. He will then show faith in us by answering our prayers and making us living examples of his divine power, providence, healing, and prosperity.

God wants faithful, reliable saints. He does not answer prayers right away is to test our character, proving who we are and what we are willing to become.

> *"Blessed is the man who remains steadfast under trial, for when he has stood the test he will receive the crown of life, which God has*

---

[1] Isaiah 43:7, Isaiah 48:11

promised to those who love him." James 1:12 ESV

A wonderful blessing waits when we show faith in God throughout our trials. Patience, loyalty and faith greatly please God. If he simply gave us what we wanted every time we asked, we would never develop the character he wanted. *Asking, Seeking, and Knocking* in prayer is a process that not only gets us what we need, but teaches us to be faithful, reliable saints with solid Christian character.

GOD KNOWS WHAT WE NEED BEFORE WE ASK HIM

"Do not be like them, for your Father knows what you need before you ask him." Matthew 6:8 ESV

God is not just concerned with what we ask for; he is concerned with *how we ask.* God wants us to learn the proper way to ask in prayer and that why there are so many references in the Bible on *how* to pray. In Matthew 6:5-7, Jesus tells his disciples how to be more efficient in prayer by giving them the do's and don'ts. Essentially, what he is saying is "Don't show off for others because God already knows what you need before you come to him in prayer." God is omniscient, or all knowing. Years before we had an idea to pray for something, God already knew and prepared an answer. We should not focus on trying to prepare God for what we are about to ask for in prayer. We need to learn how to prepare ourselves. Our attitude needs to get in alignment with the plan and purpose of God if we want to receive answers to our prayers.

Since God knows what we need before we ask, we should pray without pretense, fear, shame or doubt, expecting to receive because we are going to have faith until he answers. We can have confidence that:

1. God knows what we are going to ask in prayer and wants to give it to us.

2. The moment we ask God for something, the blessing process begins.

3. If we ask in faith, we are going to receive it.

GOD WANTS TO ANSWER OUR PRAYERS AND INCREASE OUR JOY

"Until now you have asked nothing in my name. Ask, and you will receive, that your joy may be full." John 16:24 ESV

God wants us to have more than happiness; he wants us to have *joy*. Webster's dictionary defines joy and happiness very differently.

Joy, n. *The passion or emotion excited by the acquisition or expectation of good; that excitement of pleasurable feelings which is caused by success, good fortune, the gratification of desire or some good possessed, or by a rational prospect of possessing what we love or desire; gladness; exultation; exhilaration of spirits. Joy is a delight of the mind, from the*

Happiness, n. *The agreeable sensations which spring from the enjoyment of good; that state of a being in which his desires are gratified, by the enjoyment of pleasure without pain; felicity; but happiness usually expresses less than felicity, and felicity less than bliss. Happiness is comparative. To a person distressed with pain, relief from that pain affords happiness; in other*

consideration of the present or assured approaching possession of a good. cases, we give the name happiness to positive pleasure or an excitement of agreeable sensations. Happiness therefore admits of indefinite degrees of increase in enjoyment, or gratification of desires. Perfect happiness, or pleasure unalloyed with pain, is not attainable in this life.

Joy, is associated with passion, emotional excitement and is a state of mind based on what we have already acquired or expect to acquire. Happiness, on the other hand, is associated with temporary gratification of sensations or absence of distress and suffering. Happiness is short term while joy is a longer lasting, state of mind that brings deeper pleasure because we can expect and depend on it. Jesus wants to give us long lasting joy, providing a pleasurable existence in this life and in the world to come.

"I came that they may have life and have it abundantly." John 10:10 ESV

Like any good parent, our heavenly Father wants his children to have a joyful, abundant, peaceful existence rather than lack, pain and suffering. The Bible entreats us often to ask our heavenly Father for the things we need in prayer because he wants to give us so much. God wants to give and we want to receive. What a perfect match!

"If you then, who are evil, know how to give good gifts to your children, how much more will your Father who is in heaven give good things to those who ask him!" Matthew 7:11 ESV

We have an all-powerful, all knowing, all loving father who wishes to outperform every earthly father by showering us with blessings when we ask in prayer. Let us put his promises to the test by asking for the things he wants us to have so we can have the complete joy he wants us to have.

HOW GOD ANSWERS OUR PRAYER IS TIED TO HOW HIS POWER WORKS IN US

"Now to him who is able to do far more abundantly than all that we ask or think, according to the power at work within us." Ephesians 3:20 ESV

God is all-powerful and all knowing, but he is limited by what we *allow* his power to do in our lives. God can easily move mountains, but moving people is harder. We must allow God's power to work in us by being obedient and submissive to his will. The blessings of God come easily when we allow his power to work in our lives, but slowly when we resist. When we say yes to God's will and allow him to work through us, he will do abundantly than all we ask or think.

> *"So shall my word be that goes out from my mouth; it shall not return to me empty, but it shall accomplish that which I purpose, and shall succeed in the thing for which I sent it." Isaiah 55:11 ESV*

When God speaks, blessing, prosperity, healing, and deliverance go out from his mouth and will only manifest in our lives *if we allow them to.* When the minister preaches, we have to obey the God inspired words so they will accomplish the Father's purpose in our lives. When the Holy Spirit speaks to us, we have to obey his urging so God's Word will accomplish its purpose in our life. When we read the Bible and it speaks to our heart, we have to obey so God's Word will accomplish its purpose in our life. Prayers will be answered and blessings will flow when we become used to obeying.

Allowing God's Spirit to work in us releases his power and glory. By saying "Yes Lord," we allow him to do abundantly more than we originally asked or thought. Did you get that? The Bible says God can do more than we ask or think. The more willing and obedient servants we are, the more God takes our request and does more than we originally asked. When our service and commitment exceeds God's expectations, we can expect his service and commitment to exceed our expectations. God wants to exceed our expectations in prayer because he knows that the more we receive, the more excited we will become.

The more excited we become, the more we will tell others, and the more God will receive the glory, honor and praise. The scriptures tell us we do not serve and average God, but one of abundance:

> *"And Moses lifted up his hand and struck the rock with his staff twice, and water came out **abundantly**, and the congregation drank, and their livestock." Numbers 20:11 ESV*

> *"How precious is your steadfast love, O God! The children of mankind take refuge in the shadow of your wings. They feast on the **abundance** of your house, and you give them drink from the river of your delights." Psalms 36:7-8 ESV*

> *"Man ate of the bread of the angels; he sent them food in **abundance**." Psalms 78:25 ESV*

> *"I will **abundantly** bless her provisions; I will satisfy her poor with bread." Psalms 132:15 ESV*

> *"Let the wicked forsake his way, and the unrighteous man his thoughts; let him return to the LORD, that he may have compassion on him, and to our God, for he will **abundantly** pardon." Isaiah 55:7 ESV*

*"Bring the full tithe into the storehouse, that there may be food in my house. And thereby put me to the test, says the LORD of hosts, if I will not open the windows of heaven for you and **pour down for you a blessing until there is no more need.**" Malachi 3:10 ESV*

*"The thief comes only to steal and kill and destroy. I came that they may have life and have it **abundantly.**" John 10:10 ESV*

I strive to give God more than average service because he has never been average to me. I have known him only in abundance . . . abundant in love, abundant in healing, abundant in mercy, grace, and blessings. The Bible is emphatic that God promises to bless his people with more than they need and ask for. Abraham asked for a son and God made his descendants like sand on the seashore and stars in the sky. Hannah prayed for a son and God gave her a son and a great prophet. Peter wanted to catch fish and Jesus filled the nets until they broke. From Genesis to Revelation, God cures the incurable, raises the dead, moves mountains and exceeds our wildest dreams . . . through the power of prayer. Abundant blessing is a promised result of allowing the power of God to work through us. Children of God are not confined by natural boundaries and human potential. No, for us, the supernatural becomes natural and the unreachable becomes reachable in prayer because God performs the work, not us.

> "But we have this treasure in jars of clay, to show that the surpassing power belongs to God and not to us. We are afflicted in every way, but not crushed; perplexed, but not driven to despair; persecuted, but not forsaken; struck down, but not destroyed; always carrying in the body the death of Jesus, so that the life of Jesus may also be manifested in our bodies." 2 Corinthians 4:7-10 ESV

PRAY WITH PURPOSE

*"I will say to the north, Give up, and to the south, Do not withhold; bring my sons from afar and my daughters from the end of the earth, everyone who is called by my name, **whom I created for my glory, whom I formed and made.**" Isaiah 43:6-7 ESV*

*"You did not choose me, but I chose you **and appointed you that you should go and bear fruit and that your fruit should abide,** so that whatever you ask the Father in my name, he may give it to you." John 15:16 ESV*

*"And this is **the confidence that we have toward him, that if we ask anything according to his will he hears us.** And if we know that he hears us in whatever we ask, we know that we have the requests that we have asked of him." 1 John 5:14-15 ESV*

God created humanity with purpose. Each of us must discover our God-given purpose in prayer so we can:

1. Glorify our creator by fulfilling the role in the kingdom of God that we were created for.[2]
2. Bear spiritual fruit.[3]
3. Develop the ability to ask for anything in God's will and have it fulfilled.[4]

When we begin seeking God to discover and fulfill our role in his kingdom, he will reveal the upper and lower limits of what we can obtain in prayer. Understanding what prayers God will and will not answer is important so we:

---

[2] Isaiah 43:7
[3] John 15:16
[4] 1 John 5:14-15

1. Will not be disappointed when God does not answer some prayers.
2. Learn to maximize potential blessings by asking for as much as God is willing to give us.

To better understand this principle, let us look at the steps involved in buying a car. The first step is determining what type of car you can afford. The car you can afford depends on your income, which in turn depends on your job. The next step involves submitting an application, which the car dealer uses to request a credit report and determine your line of credit. The car dealer then uses your approved credit line, occupation and down payment to determine what type of car you can afford. When asking in prayer, we must know our spiritual occupation, credit limit and down payment to determine the minimum and maximum God will give us in prayer. Our spiritual occupation could be prayer warrior, soul winner, evangelist, pastor, or whatever God has called us to be. The down payment would be the price you are willing to pay to receive what you ask for, such as hours and days spent praying or fasting. Knowing what we price we are willing to pay for results is an important because in John 15:16, Jesus says, "I chose you and appointed you that you should go and bear fruit and that your fruit should abide, so whatever you ask the Father in my name, he may give it to you." Jesus, chose his disciples, or gave them a job, to work and produce results for him. The disciples could ask the Father for anything with the guarantee they would receive because they worked for Christ. The one-hundred percent guarantee Jesus gives to answer prayer is a job benefit tied to our service for Jesus.

Praying with purpose ensures that we are focused on fulfilling God's divine plan, thereby making Jesus responsible to give us the things we need to accomplish that plan. For example, if Bob's Widget Company hired us, the employer needs to provide tools to accomplish our assigned job. If we worked in the sales department, the company needs to provide an office, cell phone, company car, computer and other necessary items to help us sell widgets. If we assembled widgets, the company needs to provide safety equipment, parts and other tools to create widgets. Hiring employees without supplying them with the necessary tools to perform their duties would be irresponsible of Bob's Widget Company. God is not irresponsible. He is not only willing, but compelled to provide what we need to fulfill our role in his kingdom bring glory to his name. We need not beg God for what we lack in life, only remind him of how willing we are to glorify him by fulfilling the role he created us for when he supplies our needs.

> *"And my God will supply every need of yours according to his riches in glory in Christ Jesus." Philippians 4:19 ESV*

Motivated by God-given purpose and knowing my needs will be met, there is no need for me to worry. My responsibility is ensuring that serving God is the focus of my life. God's responsibility is supplying our needs according to his riches and glory. To make serving him even better, Jesus often goes beyond simply supplying what we need and adds extra perks for a job well done.

> *"But seek first the kingdom of God and his righteousness, and all these things will be added to you." Matthew 6:33 ESV*

WHAT IS YOUR SPIRITUAL IDENTITY IN THE KINGDOM OF GOD?

Most people identify themselves by their chosen career. We think of ourselves as engineers, secretaries, doctors, and lawyers, but who are we spiritually? Knowing our spiritual identity is crucial if we want to understand what our prayer potential is. I define prayer potential as the maximum blessings we can ask for in prayer. For example, would a janitor working at Bob's Widget Company be able to get a company car? (I love widgets!) Probably not. Why would janitors need company cars to clean buildings? However, it does make sense to provide salesman with company cars since they frequently need to travel and sell products. If you are praying for God to bless you with a vehicle, give him a reason to do so. Tell God your plans to use what he gives you to bless the kingdom of God and bring him glory. By stating your purpose and plans, you remind God that he has a stake in answering your prayers because you, he and the kingdom of God will benefit.

Our spiritual role relates to our financial well-being because we need finances to do the work of God. We need to ask God to bless us according to the work we need to do for him. A good example would be employee salary. The difference in salary at Bob's Widget Company would probably vary depending on the jobs workers performed. Engineers would not be paid the same as secretaries. Salespeople would be paid differently from janitors, and would probably have incentive based salaries that increase with the more products they sell. The Bible tells us that God takes good financial care of his people:

> "The young lions suffer want and hunger; but those who seek the LORD lack no good thing." Psalms 34:10 ESV
>
> "But his delight is in the law of the LORD, and on his law he meditates day and night. He is

*like a tree planted by streams of water that yields its fruit in its season, and its leaf does not wither. In all that he does, he prospers."
Psalms 1:2-3 ESV*

"Praise the LORD! Blessed is the man who fears the LORD, who greatly delights in his commandments! His offspring will be mighty in the land; the generation of the upright will be blessed. Wealth and riches are in his house, and his righteousness endures forever." Psalms 112:1-3 ESV

The Bible gives us abundant evidence that God has a place and blessing for everyone willing to work in his kingdom. He takes care of those who make their primary identity as servants in the kingdom of God. Despite high unemployment and dire economic circumstances in our natural world, the kingdom of God is full of opportunities and abundant financial rewards. The kingdom of God has a surplus of jobs.

"And he said to them, "The harvest is plentiful, but the laborers are few. Therefore pray earnestly to the Lord of the harvest to send out laborers into his harvest. Luke 10:2 ESV

Many people are afraid they cannot live up to who God wants them to be spiritually. Moses felt the same way when God called him to lead the children of Israel out of Egypt when he was eighty.[5] Like Moses, God will be our partner and help us accomplish all he has called us to do because there is a lack of God-fearing laborers in the kingdom of God.[6] Our job is Ask, Seek, and Knock in prayer to get the faith, knowledge, anointing, resources and confidence to fulfill our role in God's plan. The same God that created us can create a path for us to accomplish his will. God turned Moses, a shepherd, into a spiritual shepherd of millions of souls who led his people out of slavery and to The Promised Land. God turns foul mouth fishermen into preachers and fishers of souls,[7] sinful tax collectors into collectors of souls,[8] persecutors into evangelists,[9] and humble maidens into queens and saviors.[10] What will God do when you begin to pray with purpose?

---

[5] Exodus 3:11
[6] Exodus 3:12
[7] Matthew 4:18-19
[8] Matthew 9:9
[9] Acts 9:1-16
[10] Esther 4:13-8, Esther 8:1-17

GOD'S WILL IN PRAYER

Praying with purpose also means asking in God's will. As 1 John 5:14 says, *"And this is the confidence that we have toward him, that if we ask anything according to his will he hears us."* The one-hundred percent promise to answer our prayers that Jesus makes comes into effect only when we ask according to the will of God. This means that we should want what God wants for us. God will not always give us what we want because we want it, but because he wants it for us. One of the reasons we receive random answers to prayers is because what we ask for is often not aligned with the will of God. We get frustrated when some prayers are answered but others are not. Even worse is when others receive things we desire and we begin thinking we should have them as well. When our prayers intersect with God's will and we begin fulfilling our God-given purpose, we will be much more spiritually satisfied and begin to see a substantial increase in answered prayer.

UNDERSTANDING THE IMPORTANCE OF WHO, WHAT, WHERE, WHEN AND WHY IN PRAYER

It may seem silly, but discussing *Who, What, Where, When and Why* in prayer can prove extremely valuable. When we pray, we should tell God:

1. ***Who*** – Let God know who the object of your prayer is. Is it for you or someone else?

2. ***What*** - Discuss what you are praying for in detail.

3. ***Where*** - Let God know where your prayer needs to be answered. Do you need him to work on your job, in your church, overseas, or in a family member's home? Be specific.

4. ***When*** - Timing may not always be important, but sometimes it is everything. Are you dealing with a situation where a bill needs to be paid by a certain date? Is someone's health

failing and they need immediate healing? While we cannot rush God, there are definitely times when we need him to respond quickly. David often prayed and told the Lord he was in trouble and needed help immediately.[11] When Pharaoh and the Egyptian army were close to recapturing Moses and the Israelites, Moses needed an immediate response. He prayed and God parted the Red Sea.[12] The day was ending and Joshua prayed that the sun would stand still so he could finish pursuing his enemies.[13] Urgent circumstances require urgent prayers and responses.

5. **Why** - Tell God why you need him to answer your prayer. Is your cause just? Are many souls at stake? Will the answer to your prayer result in greater glory for

---

[11] Psalm 69:17, 102:2, 143:7
[12] Exodus 14:8-31
[13] Joshua 10:12-14

the kingdom of God? Many great people in the Bible persuaded God to move on their behalf, and so can you. Abraham bargained with God at Sodom. Moses prayed often for an angry God to have mercy on the sins of the Israelites. Elijah looked to the heavens and convinced God to change the heart of Israel by raining fire from heaven and performing one miracle after the next. Passion, persuasion, and praise in prayer moves God to move mountains. James 5:16 tells us the prayer of a righteous person has a great effect on God. By giving God, and even ourselves, a just cause to rally behind, victory is more easily attained. Having a just cause is why an unknown shepherd named David defeated Goliath while King Saul hid in the trenches.[14] Learn to tell God why you need him to answer prayers and you will

---

[14] 1 Samuel 17:29

continuously walk in victory, casting a
shadow from here to eternity.

To further explain the importance of *Who, What,
Where, When and Why* in prayer, let's use the
example of applying for a bank loan again. Anyone
applying for a loan has to answer the basic
questions: who, what, where, when, and why. The
bank wants to know who the loan applicant is,
what the loan will be used for, where the person
applying for the loan lives, when the person needs
the loan, and why the loan is needed. Leaving out
that basic information will probably cause the loan
to be denied. The information provided on the
application gives the financial institution what they
need to make an informed decision about
transferring their resources. The applicant hopes
to receive money to get what they need or want
while the lender knows they will receive a satisfied
customer and interest in the future. Even though
both parties benefit from the arrangement, the
applicant has the responsibility of convincing the
lender to provide what they need. Since God

already knows what we need, we should know that he delight not only in hearing our prayer, but in how we frame the request. Listen to David's application for blessing in his prayer:

> "A Prayer of David. Hear a just cause, O LORD; attend to my cry! Give ear to my prayer from lips free of deceit! From your presence let my vindication come! Let your eyes behold the right! You have tried my heart, you have visited me by night, you have tested me, and you will find nothing; I have purposed that my mouth will not transgress. With regard to the works of man, by the word of your lips I have avoided the ways of the violent. My steps have held fast to your paths; my feet have not slipped. I call upon you, for you will answer me, O God; incline your ear to me; hear my words. Wondrously show your steadfast love, O Savior of those who seek refuge from their adversaries at your right hand. Keep me as the apple of your eye; hide me in the shadow of your wings, from the wicked who do me violence, my deadly enemies who surround me." Psalms 17:1-9 ESV

In Psalm 17:1-9, David tells God who he is, asks that his prayer be heard, praises God and gives background information on what he has done for God, then says what he needs God to do for him. This masterfully crafted prayer separates him from the ordinary person who simply prays, "Lord help me." The Psalms are a wonderful resource for anyone wanting to learn how to convince God to answer prayer. I remember being unemployed for a while and going to a job interview. I sat in front of the manager's desk, staring at a stack of nearly one hundred applicants. The manager leaned back in his chair, smiled and said, "Now tell me why I should hire you instead of any of these people." I smiled back, remembering my prayer leading up to the interview and confidently told him why I was the best candidate. He hired me that day. Getting what we need from God is not just about asking, it is about *how* we ask. Our passion, persuasion, and praise moves God to move mountains. During the winter, there are people who specialize in snow removal. The fall has people who remove leaves, while the summer has grass removal specialist. The kingdom of God needs mountain movers - people who specialize in the impossible prayers that move mountains.[15]

MORE THAN ONE PERSON CAN PRAY FOR THE SAME THING

"Again I say to you, if two of you agree on earth about anything they ask, it will be done for them by my Father in heaven. For where two or three are gathered in my name, there am I among them."
Matthew 18:19-20 ESV

In Matthew 6:1-4, Jesus says that we should spend the majority of our time in prayer away from others so we can build an intimate relationship with the Father, but he also says there are times when we need to enlist the help of others. In Matthew 18:19-20, Jesus guarantees to answer when two or more people ask for the same thing in prayer. However, Jesus makes a similar guarantee in Matthew 7:7 to those who *Ask, Seek and Knock* in prayer. If we are guaranteed results whether we pray alone or with others, what is the benefit of praying with someone else? The answer is in

---

[15] Matthew 17:20, 21:21

Matthew 18:20. When two people agree to ask for something in prayer, Jesus promises to stand with them as a guarantor or co-signer to ensure the prayer is answered. This process is better explained in the verses leading up to the discussion on group prayer in Matthew 18:15-18:

> *"If your brother sins against you, go and tell him his fault, between you and him alone. If he listens to you, you have gained your brother. But if he does not listen, take one or two others along with you, that every charge may **be established by the evidence of two or three witnesses.** If he refuses to listen to them, tell it to the church. And if he refuses to listen even to the church, let him be to you as a Gentile and a tax collector. Truly, I say to you, whatever you bind on earth shall be bound in heaven, and whatever you loose on earth shall be loosed in heaven. Matthew 18:15-18 ESV*

Jesus tells his disciples how resolve personal problems between friends by talking. If the person refuses to listen, he advises them to take two or three witnesses to and try to resolve the issue. We need help from others when we cannot resolve issues on our own. There may even be times when

God creates situations that can only be solved by involving others.

> *Two are better than one,* because they have a good reward for their toil. For if they fall, one will lift up his fellow. But woe to him who is alone when he falls and has not another to lift him up! Again, if two lie together, they keep warm, but how can one keep warm alone? And though a man might prevail against one who is alone, two will withstand him--a threefold cord is not quickly broken. *Ecclesiastes 4:9-12 ESV*

Here are advantages of two people working toward agreed objectives in prayer:

1. Two people will see results faster than one person.

2. If one person is sick, tired or unable to pray, the other person can take up the slack and ensure prayer continues.

3. Two people can work together, encouraging and keeping each other focused on the objective.

4. Defeating and discouraging two people is harder for Satan's agents than one.

5. Jesus promises to act as our witness. (Matthew 18:20) Like an expert witness testifying in court, Jesus partners with us to explain our cause to the Father and why we should receive what we are asking for.

A single strand is easily broken, but several strands tied are stronger. Together, many strands create a rope capable of bearing heavy weights that one or two could never accomplish alone. Likewise, the church is stronger when we set goals and come together focused on achieving great things. Matthew 18:18 says that we are trying to "loose" things in heaven and Earth when we pray. Some goals are easily obtained in prayer, while others need to be unlocked, such as spiritual strongholds[16] and doors that have been spiritually closed.[17] Praying with others speeds the breaking of strongholds and opening of closed doors. If you have been praying and are not making the progress

---

[16] 2 Corinthians 10:4
[17] 1 Corinthians 16:9, Colossians 4:2, Revelation 3:7-18

you need, it may be time to consider enlisting a prayer partner or group for assistance.

Here are some prominent examples of people praying together and the results:

1. Acts 1:12-14 - The Apostles and disciples of Jesus gather to "be endued with power from on high" and pray for the outpouring of the Holy Spirit.[18]

    a. 1st Result - God showed them that a twelfth, and replacement Apostle, needed to be chosen to replace Judas Iscariot.[19]

    b. 2nd Result - The group was anointed with power by receiving the gift of the Holy Spirit.[20]

    c. 3rd Result - Peter preaches the first church sermon, resulting in the

---

[18] Luke 24:49-50, Acts 1:8)
[19] Acts 1:24-26
[20] Acts 2:1-4

baptism of three-thousand people
and the establishment of the church
in Jerusalem.[21]

2. Acts 12:5 - The church prays for Peter in prison.

    a. Result - God sends an angel to free
        Peter from prison.[22]

3. Acts 13:1 - Church teachers and prophets fast and pray for Paul and Barnabas.

    a. Result - The Holy Spirit calls Paul
        and Barnabas to go on missionary
        trips where they preach the Gospel,
        perform miracles and save many
        souls.[23]

---

[21] Acts 2:38
[22] Acts 12:6-11
[23] Acts 13:2-5

PART 2 – SEEKING GOD

SEEKING GOD IS A JOURNEY OF DISCOVERY

"But, as it is written, "What no eye has seen, nor ear heard, nor the heart of man imagined, what God has prepared for those who love him"--these things God has revealed to us through the Spirit. For the Spirit searches everything, even the depths of God." 1 Corinthians 2:9-10 ESV

I believe it is important to explore the definition of seeking God. Webster's dictionary provides three definitions of the word "seek."

SEEK, v.t. pret and pp. *sought*, pronounced *sawt*. [**L.** *sequor*, to follow; for to *seek* is to go after, and the primary sense is to advance, to press, to drive forward, as in the **L.** *peto*.]

1. To go in search or quest of; to look for; to search for by going from place to place.

2. To inquire for; to ask for; to solicit; to endeavor to find or gain by any means.

3. *Seek* is followed sometimes by *out* or *after*. To *seek out*, properly implies to look for a specific thing among a number. But in general, the use of *out* and *after* with *seek*, is unnecessary and inelegant.

A closer examination of the word "seek" shows that truly seeking God involves more than taking a few minutes to ask God to do something for us in prayer. Seeking God the right way requires us to embark on a journey of discovering who God is and what he has purposed for our life. When we decide to seek God, it means that we will advance, press, and drive forward toward a spiritual goal in Christ. In seeking God, my intent is more than asking, or calling out his name, it is a determination to press forward in prayer on a mission of discovering my Creator and Savior, his divine will for my life, and the answers to my prayers. In the first definition, "seek" means "going in search or quest of; to look for; to search for by going from place to place." This means that seeking God is really a mission. Popular books and movies with quests at the center of the storyline usually involve the main character undertaking some epic, life transforming journey requiring major sacrifices, inordinate time, money and energy needed to find the objective. Seeking God is similar in that we should endeavor to launch out on a great quest to discover the God of our salvation because we know he wants to do great and mighty things through prayer.

In the second definition, the word "seek" means inquiring, soliciting and endeavoring to find by any means. This means putting our knees to ground, hearts toward heaven, and soliciting the Savior to get what we need in prayer by any means necessary in our quest of seeking God. We will not quit because we cannot quit. Many people are disappointed with prayer because when they prayed, the answer did not come quickly. We must understand that seeking God is a mission requiring more than a few hours, days or even weeks to accomplish. We must be patient and learn to trust the Lord to answer us in due time.

> *"And let us not be weary in well doing: for in due season we shall reap, if we faint not." Galatians 6:9 KJV*

Our prayers will be answered in the season God has planned, so we must wait patiently. In nature, seasons come and go at appointed times of the year. They cannot be forced. Solomon said this about seasons:

> "To every thing there is a season, and a time to every purpose under the heaven: A time to be born, and a time to die; a time to plant, and a time to pluck up that which is planted." Ecclesiastes 3:1-2 KJV

God answers prayers at a prearranged times with a prearranged purpose. We may not understand or agree with God's timing or *reasons*, but everything he does will make sense when the answer comes in the appointed *season*. Just as some seasons are long and some are short, the time we spend seeking God will vary depending on what he has planted and is *trying* to grow in us. I say "trying" because our patience determines whether spiritual growth takes place. We must condition our minds to accept and endure the situations the Lord places us in. God told Joseph he would be great one day, but I'm sure he did not feel that way when he was sold into slavery, lied on and put in prison. David was anointed the next king of Israel, but received the crown years after being declared a traitor, losing his home and family multiple times, and fighting a civil war. How often *our plans* differ from *God's timing*! Jesus guarantees he will answer our prayers, but requires we have the patience to understand how. Patience is a tool to help us bridge the gap between God's purpose and our desires.

> *"Knowing this, that the trying of your faith worketh patience. But let patience have her perfect work, that ye may be perfect and entire, wanting nothing." James 1:3-4 KJV*

Isn't it something how James describes patience as a person? He says that enduring difficult circumstances allows "Patience" to work as our trainer, molding us into the complete, godly person Christ wants us to be. We have to allow "Patience" to do her job and get us into shape! Exercise is tedious when we don't want to get in shape. Many Christians want the benefits of complete godliness without putting in the spiritual exercise. If you want answers to your prayers, **YOU MUST LEARN PATIENCE!**

SPIRITUAL GROWTH

God is not just interested in simply answering our prayers. He uses various situations in our life to teach us wisdom, patience and the will of God.

> *"I had fainted, unless I had believed to see the goodness of the LORD in the land of the living. Wait on the LORD: be of good courage, and he shall **strengthen** thine heart: wait, I say, on the LORD." Psalms 27:13-14 KJV*

Is it normal to feel like giving up at times? Yes. But we must believe in the goodness of God, trusting that he will not only answer our prayers, but strengthen us to endure any other difficult situations that may arise. When we summon the courage to be patient and wait, God gives us strength. While we are seeking the Lord and waiting for our prayers to be answered, the Holy Spirit nourishes as living water, (John 4:10, 7:38) teaches the wisdom of God, (John 14:26) and brings us into his will.

We must allow the Holy Spirit to search us if we want to learn more about God's will for us and how to receive what we ask for in prayer. The Apostle Paul describes this journey of self-discovery In 2 Corinthians 2:9-10:

> *"But, as it is written, "What no eye has seen, nor ear heard, nor the heart of man imagined, what God has prepared for those who love him"--these things God has revealed to us through the Spirit.* ***For the Spirit searches*** *everything, even the depths of God."* *1 Corinthians 2:9-10 ESV*

1. In 1 Corinthians 2:9, the Apostle Paul is telling us that God has prepared treasures for those who love him. The challenge for us is to be patient and diligent enough to find that treasure.

2. The things God has prepared for us are revealed to us through the Holy Spirit. Every Spirit filled Christian should use the Holy Spirit as a guide to find what God has prepared for them. When we take time to pray and seek God, the Holy Spirit will tell us what we need to do. We should be asking ourselves:

A. Who is it that God wants me to be?

B. What does he want me to do in the kingdom of God?

C. What spiritual and earthly blessings are waiting for me to claim? These blessings are so wonderful that the Apostle Paul says it is impossible to describe them with human eyes, ears, or imagination. With such gifts waiting for us, how can we leave them unclaimed?

3. 1 Corinthians 2:10 talks about "the depths of God." If we want to discover these depths, then we must allow the Holy Spirit to take us deeper. The depths of God contain precious spiritual gifts which allow the Lord to use us in wondrous miracles and displays of power. (1 Corinthians 12) The depths of God contain the wisdom and power used by great prophets and Apostles like

Moses, Elijah, Elisha, Peter, and Paul.
Most precious goods are hidden in the
Earth and require considerable efforts to
dig them out. Oil, gas, silver, gold,
diamonds – valuable commodities
requiring great effort and refinement to
retrieve, but once gathered, are in high
demand. What spiritual commodities are
we willing to seek in prayer to drive this
world to change? What precious gold
and diamonds wait as we go deep with
God and discover his many blessings?
Envision yourself praying, confident that
what you seek, you will find. Go deep
with God and your life and those you
love will never be the same.

*"For who knows a person's thoughts
except the spirit of that person, which is
in him? So also no one comprehends the
thoughts of God except the Spirit of God.
Now we have received not the spirit of the
world, but the Spirit who is from God, that
we might understand the things freely*

given us by God." 1 Corinthians 2:11-12 ESV

1. 1 Corinthians 2:11 says that a person really does not know what is inside their mind, but the Holy Spirit inside them does. Remarkable! We do not fully understand who we are and why we do the things we do, but we have the key to understanding those things, the Holy Spirit.

2. 1 Corinthians 2:11 also says that the Holy Spirit allows us to understand the mind of God. Understanding God's will can be difficult, but fortunately, we have the Holy Spirit to help us. The Holy Spirit helps us understand why we are not receiving the things we need in prayer. We might want to ask, "Lord, I haven't received that one million dollars I prayed for last week. Any reason why?" I'm sure he would have no problem telling us.

3. 1 Corinthians 2:12 says that God gives us the Holy Spirit to help us understand the

things freely given to us by God. Learning to allow the Holy Spirit to guide us toward God's gifts is crucial. If you have not received the gift of the Holy Spirit, then you should pray for God to fill you with his Spirit to help you understand how to obtain his blessings.

"And we impart this in words not taught by human wisdom but taught by the Spirit, interpreting spiritual truths to those who are spiritual. The natural person does not accept the things of the Spirit of God, for they are folly to him, and he is not able to understand them because they are spiritually discerned." 1 Corinthians 2:13-14 ESV

1. 1 Corinthians 2:13-14 describes how the Holy Spirit teaches us and is similar to what Jesus says in John 14:26:

*"But the Helper, the Holy Spirit, whom the Father will send in my name, he will **teach** you all things and bring to your remembrance all that I have said to you." John 14:26 ESV*

God has given us his Holy Spirit as a helper. He tutors and provides spiritual counsel so that we can receive everything God wants us to have from his Word. We should ask the Holy Spirit to show us God's spiritual truths, promises for blessings, and his divine will contained in the Bible. We should also ask him to speak his will into our mind clearly so we can understand.

2. Verse 13 says the Holy Spirit shows spiritual truths to spiritual people. If we want God to teach us and reveal those truths, then we must get in the spirit and become more spiritual. Verse 14 says the natural person cannot understand spiritual things. Spiritual things do not make sense to those who do not have the Spirit of God and use it as their primary source of help. Non-spiritual people rely on their ability to solve life's mysteries without God. Many things in life can only discerned through spiritual lenses. How many times do we come across

situation we do not understand and try to solve it without seeking God? We do not have to make our spiritual journey alone. God is available to help, interpret, and counsel, whatever we need him to do.

The spiritual person judges all things, but is himself to be judged by no one. "For who has understood the mind of the Lord so as to instruct him?" But we have the mind of Christ. 1 Corinthians 2:15-16 ESV

1 Corinthians 2:15-16 tells us that a spiritual person can discern all things. Through prayer, we can discover what God wants to do in our lives. The Holy Spirit gives us the advantage of knowing the mind of Christ so we can make sound decisions based on the will of God. He is a spiritual GPS, if you will, guiding and ensuring that we stay on the correct path in our journey of seeking God in prayer.

SEEKING GOD IS PART OF A JOURNEY

Seeking God is like taking a journey. If we want to understand the proper way to seek God and receive answers to our prayers, we have to understand what is involved in taking a journey. Every journey has four parts:

1. **Asking**. When planning to visit someone, it is normal to contact him or her in advance to make them aware of your plans so they can make the proper arrangements for your arrival. When we let God know that we are planning to seek him, we are signifying our commitment to prayer and knowing him.

2. **Preparation.(Part of Seeking)** Preparation is the first part, or planning phase of seeking God. It involves knowing where you are going, how you will get there, and how much it will cost. In seeking God, you need to consider how much time to spend in prayer, fasting, and Bible study. What will you do if you encounter obstacles? How committed are you to the journey and how

far are you willing to go to get what you need in prayer? Planning and preparation are crucial when seeking God if you want to reach your destination.

3. **Taking the Journey. (Seeking)** The journey of seeking God begins when we start seeking God with prayer, fasting, studying the Bible and obeying the will of God.

4. **The Arrival. (Knocking)** At the end of a journey, the traveler arrives at the destination and makes their presence known. When we arrive at the end of our spiritual journey, we must *knock* and claim the answer to our prayers. Many people assume that after weeks, months and years of prayer, the answer will show up one day and when it does not, they become disappointed and disillusioned. We have to learn what it means to *knock* in prayer. Not knowing is like arriving at someone's house and standing at the front door without

knocking or ringing the bell, waiting for an answer that may never come. If we want to receive guaranteed results in prayer then we must understand what the Bible says about *knocking* and why it is so essential. We will examine Preparation in the next chapter.

PREPARING FOR THE JOURNEY

"Whoever does not bear his own cross and come after me cannot be my disciple. For which of you, desiring to build a tower, does not first sit down and count the cost, whether he has enough to complete it?" Luke 14:27-28 ESV

If we want to be successful followers of Christ, we must learn to "count the cost," which means preparing for our spiritual journey. Jesus knew the Christian walk would be filled with ups and downs, happiness and heartache, trials and tribulation. Jesus taught his disciples the importance of planning for success because of what they would experience. Our lives would be easier if we spent more time planning rather than living the haphazard way most of us do now. We tend to pray when we need something from God or experience trials. As a result, our prayer lives tend to be knee-jerk, emotional responses to stress rather than pre-planned, purpose driven prayers that invoke results. An organized, well thought plan will always succeed more than disorganized, impulse driven attempts at resolving issues.

Behind every successful enterprise is a successful plan. If we want more success in prayer, then we must stop *finding time to pray* and *schedule time to pray*. When someone wants to travel by airplane, the first thing they do is check the flight schedule. If the airlines did not publish flight schedules and flew whenever they chose, how could they be relied upon as a dependable mode of transportation? Reliability is as necessary in prayer as it is in business. We should strive to build a consistent prayer life by scheduling time to seek God with the intent of achieving guaranteed results. Here are some quotes about the importance of planning:

> *"By failing to prepare, you are preparing to fail."* - Benjamin Franklin
> *"Few people have a next; they live from hand to mouth without a plan, and are always at the end of their line."* - Ralph Waldo Emerson

"Planning without action is futile. Action without planning is fatal." Unknown.

"To be prepared is half the victory." Miguel de Cervantes (Spanish novelist)

The reason behind so many unanswered prayers is a failure to prepare. Most people resort to prayer only in times of distress and when the answer does not come, they become bitter or disappointed. We have to understand that God not only wants to answer prayers, he wants to build a relationship with us. Unfortunately, most people just want an answer to prayer, not a relationship. The Lord wants to do more than listen to our complaints, wish lists, and groaning about when he is going to answer us. When we schedule time to pray and seek the Lord, it shows God that we are not trying to use him for what he can do for us, but we want a genuine relationship with him.

Miguel de Cervantes said, *"To be prepared is half the victory."* This quote is very important because ultimately, we want victorious prayer lives where we receive the things we ask for. David taught Solomon his son and the elders of Israel the importance of preparing to seek God.

> *"David also commanded all the leaders of Israel to help Solomon his son, saying, "Is not the LORD your God with you? And has he not given you peace on every side? For he has delivered the inhabitants of the land into my hand, and the land is subdued before the LORD and his people. **Now set your mind and heart to seek the LORD your God.** Arise and build the sanctuary of the LORD God, so that the ark of the covenant of the LORD and the holy vessels of God may be brought into a house built for the name of the LORD.""* 1 Chronicles 22:17-19 ESV

Solomon was the wisest and wealthiest person in history. He was extremely diligent in planning and organizing every part of his life, including the spiritual and natural. In 1 Chronicles 22:17-19, David charges Solomon to "set his mind and heart to seek the Lord his God." David is telling his son, "Solomon, you are going to be a king and very important person, but if you want to truly be successful, make seeking God and building the house of the Lord the most important things in your life." Psalms, Proverbs and Ecclesiastes tell of Solomon's deep desire for the wisdom of God, indicating that he was devoted to seeking God. His devotion is eventually rewarded. In 1 Kings 3:5, God appears to Solomon and says, "Ask what I shall give you." 1 Kings 3:5 and Matthew 7:7 are very similar:

> *"**Ask, and it will be given to you;** seek, and you will find; knock, and it will be opened to you.*
> *Matthew 7:7 ESV*
>
> *At Gibeon the LORD appeared to Solomon in a dream by night, and God said, "**Ask what I shall give you.**" 1 Kings 3:5 ESV*

Both promise guaranteed answers to prayer resulting from guaranteed time spent with God in prayer. When we develop an intimate relationship with God, *he will seek us out* and confirm that we have graduated from *grasping* to *guarantees* in prayer. Grasping is where we pray and *hope* God answers us. Guarantees are when *God confirms* he will answer our prayers, sometimes even before we ask.

Start preparing your heart to seek God by making a plan. I encourage you to use the free materials available on my website to schedule time for prayer or you can create your own. By scheduling time for prayer, fasting and Bible Study, you will develop a more intimate relationship with the Lord. You prayers will change from one-way request to two-way conversations. Make time for the Lord as anyone in a healthy relationship would and you may find the Lord eagerly approaching you outside your scheduled times, as he did with Solomon, to tell you about all he wants to give you.

SEEKING GOD EARLY

"I love them that love me; and those that seek me early shall find me." Proverbs 8:17 KJV

Understanding the significance of Morning Prayer is necessary if you want to experience major breakthroughs in prayer. Proverbs 8:17 is another of those *guarantee scriptures*, promising that if you seek God early, he will meet you. The odds of receiving answers to prayer are very good any time you pray, but the chances increase dramatically when you seek God early *because of the guarantee*. Seeking God early in prayer sends a message about your sincerity and willingness to go beyond what the average person does. The Bible tells us that when people are in trouble and serious about seeking God, they will seek him early:

> *"When your fear cometh as desolation, and your destruction cometh as a whirlwind; when distress and anguish cometh upon you. Then shall they call upon me, but I will not*

*answer; **they shall seek me early,** but they shall not find me:" Proverbs 1:27-28 KJV*

*"I will go and return to my place, till they acknowledge their offence, and seek my face: in their affliction **they will seek me early**." Hosea 5:15 KJV*

God knows that when we are serious about finding him, we will seek him early in the morning because doing so conveys our conviction and commitment.

People serious about getting results seek God early in prayer. Here are some examples:

Jacob
*"And Jacob **rose up early in the morning**, and took the stone that he had put for his pillows, and set it up for a pillar, and poured oil upon the top of it. And he called the name of that place Bethel: but the name of that city was called Luz at the first." Genesis 28:18-19 KJV*

Moses
*"And he hewed two tables of stone like unto the first; and Moses **rose up early in the morning**, and went up unto mount Sinai, as the LORD had commanded him, and took in his hand the two tables of stone. And the LORD descended in the cloud, and stood with*

him there, and proclaimed the name of the LORD." Exodus 34:4-5 KJV

Hezekiah

*"Then Hezekiah the king **rose early**, and gathered the rulers of the city, and went up to the house of the LORD." 2 Chronicles 29:20 KJV*

Job

*"And it was so, when the days of their feasting were gone about, that Job sent and sanctified them, and **rose up early in the morning**, and offered burnt offerings according to the number of them all: for Job said, It may be that my sons have sinned, and cursed God in their hearts. Thus did Job continually." Job 1:5 KJV*

Jesus

*"And **in the morning, rising up a great while before day**, he went out, and departed into a solitary place, and there prayed." Mark 1:35 KJV*

David

*"My voice shalt thou hear in the morning, O LORD; **in the morning** will I direct my prayer unto thee, and will look up." Psalms 5:3 KJV*

The Apostles and Disciples

*"For these people are not drunk, as you suppose, since it is only **the third hour**[24] of the day." Acts 2:15 ESV*

When you are serious and determined to get results in prayer, an innate desire to commune with God will rouse your soul to pray early:

"My heart is fixed, O God, my heart is fixed: I will sing and give praise. Awake up, my glory; awake, psaltery and harp: I myself will awake early." Psalms 57:7-8 KJV

Psalm 57 was written when David was in the wilderness, desperate and hiding from King Saul. In deep trouble and fearing for his life, David sought God earnestly, rising early to praise and worship his Savior.

Jacob was also in a desperate situation at Peniel when he needed God to prevent his brother Esau from killing him.[25]

"And Jacob was left alone. And a man wrestled with him until the breaking of the day. When the man saw that he did not prevail against Jacob, he touched his hip

---

[24] The 3rd hour of the day is 9:00 AM
[25] Genesis 32:7-32

socket, and Jacob's hip was put out of joint as he wrestled with him. Then he said, "Let me go, for the day has broken." But Jacob said, "I will not let you go unless you bless me." And he said to him, "What is your name?" And he said, "Jacob." Then he said, "Your name shall no longer be called Jacob, but Israel, for you have striven with God and with men, and have prevailed."" Genesis 32:24-28 ESV

Jacob was going to meet Esau the next morning. Esau had four hundred armed men and had sworn to kill Jacob the next time they met because of the devious ways Jacob had swindled him out of an inheritance and blessing when they were younger. But something strange happens. God appears to Jacob as a man and gives him the opportunity to *wrestle* for a blessing. Alone, outnumbered, and desperate, Jacob accepts the challenge and wins. We learn several important things from this story:

1. **The more determined you are in prayer, the more likely you are to receive what you are asking for.** God is impressed by people who use cunning and diligence to obtain spiritual blessings. Jacob often used

guile to obtain spiritual treasures others saw as trash. Although his methods were controversial, Jacob swayed God because he was determined to be blessed. God is impressed when the righteous have enough faith to fight for what they want.[26]

2. **God did not want to change Jacob's situation, he wanted to change Jacob.** Genesis 32:1 says the angels of God met him earlier at Mahanaim, meaning Jacob had God's protection. Although he had protection, Jacob lacked *confidence in that protection.* He was fine when surrounded by visible signs that God was with him, but when the angels disappeared, so did his faith. To have lasting faith, Jacob needed more than protection; he needed *courage.* He needed the courage to trust God and

---

[26] Matthew 15:22-28 – A Canaanite woman pleads for her daughter to be delivered from an evil spirit. Luke 18:2-8 – An elderly widow refuses to give up until she receives justice.

walk by faith, not by sight.[27]

3. **We gain strength and confidence as we wrestle and pray.** God touched Jacob's hip, *weakening his body, but strengthening his soul.* As Jacob wrestled with the angel of the Lord, he wrestled with his fears and doubts. Jacob's victory against the angel taught him that he could overcome any situation if he refused to give up. In the morning, Jacob faced the *same problem*, but with a *different attitude.* He met Esau believing that no problem is too big for God.

*For his anger is but for a moment, and his favor is for a lifetime. Weeping may tarry for the night, **but joy comes with the morning.** As for me, I said in my prosperity, "I shall never be moved." Psalms 30:5-6 ESV*

Victory comes in the morning. Be there to receive it.

---

[27] 2 Corinthians 5:7 Luke 18:2-8 – An elderly widow refuses to give up until she receives justice.

If you want to increase the chances of your prayers being answered, take the initiative and start seeking God early.

> *A Psalm of David, when he was in the wilderness of Judah. O God, thou art my God; early will I seek thee: my soul thirsteth for thee, my flesh longeth for thee in a dry and thirsty land, where no water is; Psalms 63:1 KJV*

While being pursued by men, David *pursued God*. No one had to encourage him; he rose early to pray, driven by an innate desire to seek God. David seemed spiritually and physically affected when he could not to seek the solace of God's presence. His soul was thirsty, and needed to be quenched by the Living Waters of the Holy Spirit.[28] The more you are filled by the Spirit, the more you want to be filled. Being in God's presence becomes necessary, an addiction of the spirit to the Spirit, where your soul can only be nourished by the presence of God:

> *"With my soul have I desired thee in the night; yea, with my spirit within me will I*

---

[28] John 4:10, 7:38

seek thee early: for when thy judgments are in the earth, the inhabitants of the world will learn righteousness." Isaiah 26:9 KJV

Those filled by the Spirit are compelled to seek God early, driven by a yearning to be in the God's presence. Do you want this kind of passion? Seek the Lord early and soon his Spirit will awaken your spirit.

HAVE A SENSE OF URGENCY

"Seek the LORD while he may be found; call upon him while he is near"; Isaiah 55:6 ESV

We have been given us an open invitation to seek the Lord. We must develop a sense of urgency and begin seeking the Lord in prayer as soon as possible because the invitation he has given us will expire. God hears every prayer at every moment and answers them at a time and place of his choosing. But, there are times when he comes closer, and makes his desire to work with and through us clearer. This is often labeled *The Call of God.* We need to respond quickly in these unique times when God is calling us because our response determines what type of relationship we will have with the Lord and how quickly he will answer our prayers.

Most people either ignore God's calling or misinterpret what he is trying to do in their lives. This leads to confusion and unanswered prayers. When we don't get the message, God calls louder, or changes circumstances and situations around us. The Lord speaks to us in various ways, such as:

1. *Directly* through an audible voice.[29]

2. *Directly* through our conscience.[30]

3. *Directly* through a dream or vision.[31]

4. *Directly* through urgings of the Holy Spirit.[32]

5. *Directly* through another person giving us:

   a. Natural wisdom or knowledge

   b. Supernatural wisdom or knowledge.[33]

6. *Indirectly* through preaching, Bible Studies or biblical teaching.

7. *Indirectly* as we read the Bible.

---

[29] Exodus 3:1-4 – God speaks to Moses through a burning bush. 1 Samuel 3 – God speaks to Samuel as a child

[30] 2 Corinthians 1:12

[31] 1 Kings 3:5 – God speaks to Solomon in a dream. Acts 10:1-6 – God speaks to Cornelius in a vision.

[32] Acts 11:12 – The Holy Spirit tells Peter to go with Cornelius' servants

[33] 1 Corinthians 12:8 – The spiritual gifts of wisdom and word of knowledge. Luke 1:41-55 – The Holy Spirit anoints Elisabeth to bless Mary.

We have to respond when God is trying to get our attention because he will not reach out to us forever.

> *"But they refused to pay attention and turned a stubborn shoulder and stopped their ears that they might not hear. They made their hearts diamond-hard lest they should hear the law and the words that the LORD of hosts had sent by his Spirit through the former prophets. Therefore great anger came from the LORD of hosts.* **"As I called, and they would not hear, so they called, and I would not hear,**" *says the LORD of hosts,"* Zechariah 7:11-13 ESV

While most of us don't see ourselves as stubborn or selfish, we can admit there were times God was trying to reach us, and we ignored him. By allowing our plans to supersede the will of God, our hearts become hard as a diamond. This prevents the Word of God and the Holy Spirit from penetrating and persuading us to do the will of the Lord. If we are obedient and seek the Lord while he is near, blessing and prosperity will follow. If we choose to be disobedient, we risk rousing the

Lord's anger and when we call upon him in our distress, he may ignore us.

I have visited and prayed with people many times in trouble and called on the Lord after refusing to serve him. It was difficult because they were in dire situations and desperately reaching out for help, trying to curry God's favor. There were times when the anointing flowed and the Lord blessed wondrously, but there were also times when I struggled in intercession because the person's relationship with the Lord was not where it should have been, making it harder for them to receive an answer. Receiving what you need in prayer is far easier when the Lord is close than when he is far away. Has someone ever offered you something, and you refused, only later to realize that you needed what they offered? You desperately try contacting the person, but *now it is harder to reach them because they aren't as close.* You realize that you should have accepted when they first offered. **Now** is the time to begin seeking and serving God. Tomorrow is too late because God has been calling for so, so long. Be urgent and act now, while we are under God's grace.

> *"Let the wicked forsake his way, and the unrighteous man his thoughts; let him return to the LORD, that he may have compassion on him, and to our God, for he will abundantly pardon." Isaiah 55:7 ESV*

Many people have used the excuse, "I won't start serving God until I'm sure I won't fail him." God does not require that we get ourselves together before serving him. If we come to him now, he will have compassion and abundantly pardon our sins. We may not understand how God is going to help us turn our lives around or deliver us, but that is why he is God.

> *"For my thoughts are not your thoughts, neither are your ways my ways, declares the LORD. For as the heavens are higher than the earth, so are my ways higher than your ways and my thoughts than your thoughts. "For as the rain and the snow come down from heaven and do not return there but water the earth, making it bring forth and sprout, giving seed to the sower and bread to the eater, so shall my word be that goes out from my mouth; it shall not return to me empty,*

but it shall accomplish that which I purpose, and shall succeed in the thing for which I sent it." For you shall go out in joy and be led forth in peace; the mountains and the hills before you shall break forth into singing, and all the trees of the field shall clap their hands." Isaiah 55:8-12 ESV

God's ability to do miracles and change lives is limitless and greater than anything we can comprehend. Nothing is impossible with God. When God makes a promise, we can count on it. None of his promises will fail unless we refuse to obey his will. God **guarantees** that when we seek him, his Word will move on our behalf, giving us joy, success, peace, and causing everything around us to praise God.

SEEK GOD WITH ALL YOUR HEART, SOUL AND MIND

"Blessed are those who keep his testimonies, who seek him with their whole heart," Psalms 119:2 ESV

God wants our best. He isn't interested in halfhearted, disingenuous attempts at getting to know him. The blessings of God come when we give our best by seeking him with our whole heart. How would you feel about someone befriending you just to get something they wanted? Wouldn't you feel betrayed? Would you give them what they wanted after discovering they really didn't' care about you? Well, that is how God feels when we are insincere in our attempts to seek him in prayer.

Seeking God is not about getting what we want from God, it is about learning how to love him with sincerity. Seeking God is about learning to put God's needs first and committing all our heart, mind and soul and to serving him. Trying to receive God's blessings without giving him all our heart mind and soul is similar to robbery because we are taking something from someone we don't care about. The love and devotion we show in seeking God should match what he has shown for us.

Jesus said loving God sincerely is the most important commandment:

> *"And one of the scribes came up and heard them disputing with one another, and seeing that he answered them well, asked him, "Which commandment is the most important of all?" Jesus answered, "The most important is, 'Hear, O Israel: The Lord our God, the Lord is one. And you shall love the Lord your God* **with all your heart and with all your soul and with all your mind and with all your strength.'"** *Mark 12:28-30 ESV*

God is not asking for some of our love and devotion. He is asking for all of it. For some people, this seems impossible, even demanding. How does God expect us to devote so much time and energy to him and the church when we have such busy lives? Most people are barely finding time to pray and attend church as it is. The disciples raised similar questions about the kind of devotion Jesus expected:

*"And they were exceedingly astonished, and said to him, "Then who can be saved?" Jesus looked at them and said, "**With man it is impossible, but not with God. For all things are possible with God.**" Peter began to say to him, "See, we have left everything and followed you." Jesus said, "Truly, I say to you, there is no one who has left house or brothers or sisters or mother or father or children or lands, for my sake and for the gospel, who will not receive a hundredfold now in this time, houses and brothers and sisters and mothers and children and lands, with persecutions, and in the age to come eternal life." Mark 10:26-30 ESV*

What we think is impossible in our minds is fully possible with God. If we turn to him with questions and issues of serving and loving him, he can help. It is an issue of trust. Do we trust God enough to follow him completely? Are we willing to seek him in prayer not just for the things we understand, but for those we do not? When faced with doubts or situations seemingly beyond our control, we should do what faithful followers of Christ have always done; ask him what to do.

Jesus promised that those who follow him with their whole heart will be rewarded in this world one hundredfold and with eternal life and the next. The Lord demands a lot from us but promises tremendous blessings in return. Isn't a few hours of prayer, Bible study, church attendance, and righteous living worth a one hundredfold blessing? Most financial planners would agree that an investment yielding twice the original principle would definitely be worth taking advantage of. Increase the promised return to one-hundred fold, and you would be silly not to invest. Jesus promises a large return on the time, energy, love, devotion, and sacrifice we invest and serving him. King Hezekiah understood this principle and prospered:

> *"Thus Hezekiah did throughout all Judah, and he did what was good and right and faithful before the LORD his God. And every work that he undertook in the service of the house of God and in accordance with the law and the commandments, seeking his God, **he did with all his heart, and prospered.**" 2 Chronicles 31:20-21 ESV*

Hezekiah was a king and far busier than most of us will ever be, but he found time to seek God with all his heart, and was rewarded for it. If a king could devote himself to God, why can't we? We cannot pray like peasants and expect to be rewarded like kings. Prayers rich in love, devotion, and sacrifice produce rich results while prayers devoid of commitment produce poor results. Hezekiah's miraculous deliverance,[34] tremendous financial increase,[35] bodily healing,[36] and anointed political leadership[37] were the result of his unwavering commitment to seeking God with all his heart. Commit to God and he will commit to you.

---

[34] 2 Chronicles 32:1-23
[35] 2 Chronicles 32:27-29
[36] 2 Chronicles 32:24
[37] 2 Chronicles 32:30

PART 3 - KNOCKING

OVERCOMING OBSTACLES

"I know your works. Behold, I have set before you an open door, which no one is able to shut. I know that you have but little power, and yet you have kept my word and have not denied my name." Revelation 3:8 ESV

If we want guaranteed results in prayer, then we have to learn how to knock. Knocking is the final step in the journey of *Asking, Seeking and Knocking* and is what we must do to obtain the guaranteed rewards of answered prayer. Knocking is often necessary because before we receive an answer to great prayers, there are obstacles, (or doors) preventing us from claiming our reward. Many people pray without seeing results due to an inability to deal with obstacles.

In Revelation 3:8, Jesus tells the church of Philadelphia that he has set an open door in front of them. This is very interesting because Matthew 7:7 says, "Knock, and it shall be opened," referring to a door. "Doors" and "knocking" are symbolic representations of the final destination in the journey of *Asking, Seeking and Knocking* in prayer. If you were to take a trip to someone's house, when you arrive, you would need to *knock on the door,* and ask to be let in. The church of Philadelphia needed Jesus to open the door before they could receive the reward for their works. They went through the process of *Asking and Seeking* in prayer, and upon reaching the end of their journey, Jesus opened the door and gave them what they needed.

The last part of the journey can be the most frustrating. After arriving at the destination, we expect a warm reception, not a closed door. We knock, ring the bell, make phone calls . . . whatever it takes to get someone to open the door and get past that final obstacle. The excitement we had has turned to disappointment; maybe even anger. Weren't they expecting us? Don't they know we are uncomfortable? We feel disappointed after praying and God does not respond.

Don't let discomfort and disappointment affect your faith. If we are to receive what we ask for in prayer, we have to learn how to deal with discomfort and disappointment and continue "knocking" as Jesus instructed. Trials (or obstacles) will need to be overcome before Jesus opens the door and answers our great prayers. The church of Philadelphia is an example of knocking to get doors opened:

> *"'I know your works. Behold, I have set before you an open door, which no one is able to shut. I know that you have but little power, and yet you have kept my word and have not denied my name." Revelation 3:8 ESV*

> *"Because you have kept my word about patient endurance, I will keep you from the hour of trial that is coming on the whole world, to try those who dwell on the earth." Revelation 3:10 ESV*

Achieving guaranteed results in prayer takes patience and endurance. Jesus tells the faithful church members they were patient and enduring, having kept his word and not denying his name. History tells us that first-century Christians underwent severe persecutions and trials because of their faith. In Revelation 3:10, Jesus promised to keep them from a greater trial that would come upon the world because they endured a previous trial. We do not know what global trial the church experienced, but Jesus made sure it did not affect them. Our present trials may seem overwhelming, but in overcoming them, *we avoid greater trials in the future.*

The Israelites underwent trials after Moses came to free them from Egypt. When Moses went before Pharaoh to plead for his people's freedom, his request was denied and the people were *made to work harder.*[38] They did not realize it at the time, but everything that happened was part of God's plan to free and teach them who he was and display his awesome power. To the Israelites, it seemed like a setback. Many times we pray and the situation seems to get worse before it gets better. God allows Satan to put obstacles in our path to test our faith. Moses and the Israelites overcame trials and gained freedom, but more importantly,

---

[38] Exodus 5:1-21

they took the first step in learning to be patient and trust God.

God gave the Israelites divine protection from the plagues sent upon the Egyptians[39] because they were under his protection. They underwent hardship before deliverance arrived because they wanted to serve God, but it was nothing compared to the death, disease, and financial disasters the Egyptians later experienced. This should be a lesson for us today as we deal with tremendous global trials. As people of God with divine protection, Christians should not have to experience the same trials as those who do not serve God. Our trust should be in the Lord. The world may experience economic recession, but we don't have to. Our God is great and so is his power! He can heal,[40] deliver,[41] protect, and provide for our finances[42] just as he did with Moses and the

---

[39] Exodus 8:22-23, 9:23-26, 10:22-23
[40] Exodus 15:26
[41] Exodus 14:30-31
[42] Exodus 12:36

Israelites. We just have to show the same faith, endurance, and determination.

OUR ADVERSARY

As we ask and seek God in prayer, an adversary will try to stop us.

> *"Be sober-minded; be watchful. Your adversary the devil prowls around like a roaring lion, seeking someone to devour." 1 Peter 5:8 ESV*

The Devil and his agents work diligently to prevent us from receiving answers to our prayers. The Devil worked tirelessly to destroy the lives of Job and his family.[43] He sent demonic princes to prevent Daniel from receiving an answer to his prayer.[44] God sends angels to aid and strengthen us because Satan sends evil spirits to weaken us. We are not alone when praying and seeking God. The Devil wants us to give up. The closer we get to receive the promise, the harder he fights, because

---

[43] Job 1:6-19, 2:1-7
[44] Daniel 10:9-20

we are close to receiving. Most of us know the saying, "It's always darkest before dawn." Jesus works on our behalf while the Devil is working against us. While we are at the door knocking, Jesus encourages us to hold fast while the Devil discourages and tries to make us give up.

When Jesus finally opens the door, he will reward us for our faithful determination.

> *"Resist him, firm in your faith, knowing that the same kinds of suffering are being experienced by your brotherhood throughout the world. And after you have suffered a little while, the God of all grace, who has called you to his eternal glory in Christ, will himself restore, confirm, strengthen, and establish you." 1 Peter 5:9-10 ESV*

Christians throughout the world are suffering, but after we have suffered for a little while, (or continued knocking for a little while) God will restore, confirm strengthen and establish us. He will answer our prayers!

Everyone in the Bible who prayed, sought God, and underwent trials was wonderfully rewarded at the end. Job endured great adversity and trials by Satan, but he had a great mindset:

> "Then Job arose and tore his robe and shaved his head and fell on the ground and worshiped. And he said, "Naked I came from my mother's womb, and naked shall I return. The LORD gave, and the LORD has taken away; blessed be the name of the LORD." **In all this Job did not sin or charge God with wrong."** Job 1:20-22 ESV

> "Then his wife said to him, "Do you still hold fast your integrity? Curse God and die." But he said to her, "You speak as one of the foolish women would speak. Shall we receive good from God, and shall we not receive evil?"" **In all this Job did not sin with his lips.** Job 2:9-10 ESV

Despite his dire situation, Job did not turn his back on God because he knew God did not turn his back on him. He took the good and bad he received in stride. Years ago, I endured the greatest trial of my life - four surgeries, nearly one hundred days in the hospital, and constant sickness. Only then did I really comprehend Job's sufferings. With financial problems, sickness, friends and family questioning my walk with God, I understood why people question God. Why would he do this to me, a faithful minister and longtime servant? I refused to become bitter and blame God, although tempted many times. Like Job, when miraculous recovery came, others and I saw the grace of God in a new light as faithfulness was rewarded. I can say this with sincerity and appreciation, it is darkest before dawn, and trials do become more intense before rewards.

> *"And the LORD restored the fortunes of Job, when he had prayed for his friends. And the LORD gave Job twice as much as he had before. Then came to him all his brothers and sisters and all who had known him before, and ate bread with him in his house. And they showed him sympathy and comforted him for all the evil that the LORD had brought upon him. And each of them gave him a piece of money and a ring of gold. **And the LORD blessed the latter days of Job more than his beginning.** And he had 14,000 sheep, 6,000 camels, 1,000 yoke of oxen, and 1,000 female donkeys. He had also seven sons and three daughters. And he called the name of the first daughter Jemimah, and the name of the second Keziah, and the name of the third Keren-happuch. And in all the land there were no women so beautiful as Job's*

daughters. And their father gave them an inheritance among their brothers." Job 42:10-15 ESV

Do you want to be significantly blessed? Hold on to the end of your trial. Job's victory teaches us several important things:

1. **The key to Job's deliverance was his determination in prayer.** He could have given up and become bitter because of his situation and lack of empathy from his friends. Instead, he chose prayer and forgiveness. Giving up and being downcast is easy when things are going wrong and it seems our spiritual journey is going nowhere. The faithful Christian understands that each day traveled is a day closer to reaching the objective. Keep praying. A determined attitude keeps knocking until the door is opened, receiving restoration and great blessing.

2. **Job came out of his trial more blessed than he started.** God restored everything

Job lost *and then added more.* Great blessing come with great faith. Jesus taught this principle in Mark 10:28-30, when speaking about sacrifice:

> *Peter began to say to him, "See, we have left everything and followed you." Jesus said, "Truly, I say to you, there is no one who has left house or brothers or sisters or mother or father or children or lands, for my sake and for the gospel, who will not receive a hundredfold now in this time, houses and brothers and sisters and mothers and children and lands, with persecutions, and in the age to come eternal life. Mark 10:28-30 ESV*

When we sacrifice and faithfully follow Jesus, he restores what we lost and adds extra. I call this *"addition by subtraction."* God takes something away to give us more. When we are in a trial, the finances, family, friends, and material goods we lose seem like a great loss. After the trial, we will realize what we lost was minimal compared to the blessings God added to our life.

Keep knocking and it will be opened. Guaranteed blessings, tremendous increase, spiritual and financial blessings are just behind the door.

PART 4 - 7 DAY DEVOTIONAL

Before starting the devotion, determine what you want to ask God for and set time aside each morning and evening to study the devotion and prayer. Try to be consistent each day with your prayer and study time.

DEVOTIONAL PART 1

ASKING

DAY 1 - MORNING DEVOTION

Learning How to Pray

"And whenever you pray, don't be like the hypocrites who love to stand in the synagogues and on the street corners so that they will be seen by people. I tell you with certainty, they have their full reward! But whenever you pray, go into your room, close the door, and pray to your Father who is hidden. And your Father who sees from the hidden place will reward you. "When you are praying, don't say meaningless things like the gentiles do, because they think they will be heard by being so wordy. Don't be like them, because your Father knows what you need before you ask him." Matthew 6:5-8 ISV

Asking God for something is prayer. If we want to receive what we ask for, then we must learn how to pray properly. Jesus teaches his disciples how to pray in Matthew 6:5-13. What Jesus taught can be divided in two parts. The first part is Matthew 6:5-8, listed above) where Jesus teaches what attitude we should have in prayer. The second part is Matthew 6:9-15 (listed below)

"Therefore, this is how you should pray: 'Our Father in heaven, may your name be kept

holy. May your kingdom come. May your will be done, on earth as it is in heaven. Give us today our daily bread, and forgive us our sins, as we have forgiven those who have sinned against us. And never bring us into temptation, but deliver us from the evil one.' Because if you forgive people their offenses, your heavenly Father will also forgive you. But if you do not forgive people their offenses, your Father will not forgive your offenses."
Matthew 6:9-15 ISV

Jesus tells his disciples what topics to discuss in prayer. As you enter prayer, make an effort to have the proper attitude and talk with God about topics important to him, besides what you want so you can receive your reward.

Let's Review

1. Can you identify the two DONT'S Jesus talks about in Matthew 6:5-8?

    A.

    B.

2. Can you identify the seven important topics Jesus says we should pray about in Matthew

6:9-15? As you pray each day, be sure to discuss these items.

    A.

    B.

    C.

    D.

    E.

    F.

    G.

3. Of the five topics, which does Jesus elaborate on the most?

Now Go Pray

Find a place to pray. Take 5-10 minutes to pray the Lord's Prayer and the rest about things important to you.

Prayer Journal

Use the Journal to record your experiences during prayer. You may want to record any thoughts that

come into your mind or if you feel the Holy Spirit speaking to you.

DAY 1 - EVENING DEVOTION

Determination in Prayer

"Jesus told his disciples a parable about their need to pray all the time and never give up. He said, "In a city there was a judge who didn't fear God or respect people. In that city there was also a widow who kept coming to him and saying, 'Grant me justice against my adversary.' For a while the judge refused. But later he told himself, 'I don't fear God or respect people, yet because this widow keeps bothering me, I will grant her justice. Otherwise, she will keep coming and wear me out.'" Then the Lord added, "Listen to what the unrighteous judge says. **Won't God grant his chosen people justice when they cry out to him day and night?** *Is he slow to help them? I tell you, he will give them justice quickly. But when the Son of Man comes, will he find faith on earth?"* Luke 18:1-8 ISV

In prayer, asking is more than saying, "Lord I need this, or God I want that." When we ask God for something, we must understand that the answer will not always come right away. Yes, in

Matthew 7:7, Jesus gives a 100% guarantee to answer our prayers. But, he does not say when so we must prepare to go the distance in prayer by developing commitment and determination. Today, develop an attitude like the widow and resolve to go to God daily in prayer until we receive what we want in prayer.

Let's Review

1. Have you ever given up on God in Prayer?

2. What are the most consecutive days you have prayed for one thing?

3. Are you ready now to prayer until you receive the answer to your prayer?

Now Go Pray

Find a place to pray. Take 5-10 minutes to pray the Lord's Prayer, 5-10 minutes about determination, and the rest about things important to you.

Prayer Journal

Use the Journal to record your experiences during prayer. You may want to record any thoughts that come into your mind or if you feel the Holy Spirit speaking to you.

DAY 2 - MORNING DEVOTION

God Already Knows

"Don't be like them, because your Father knows what you need before you ask him." Matthew 6:8 ISV

"'Don't be afraid, Daniel," he told me, "because from the first day that you committed yourself to understand and to humble yourself before your God, your words were heard. I've come in answer to your prayers.'" Daniel 10:12 ISV

Today's focus will be on having faith in prayer. When we are in a difficult situation, it is hard to trust God to answer our prayer. The waiting and hoping can be nerve wracking. Consider this: God *already knows* what we need before we pray. The angel Gabriel appeared to Daniel and said his prayers were heard from the moment he committed to understand God's will. This is why commitment to what we ask for is so important.

As you pray, picture God looking at you with a smile as you approach him and then he says, "I already know what you are coming to ask me and have already begun working to deliver the answer." Understand that what you are asking for is just confirmation of what God already knows and is in the process of answering. Now, remove worry and doubt, replacing them with faith and trust that God will deliver the answer you need very soon.

Let's Review

1. How did you feel about receiving what you asked for before praying this morning?

2. How do you feel after reading the scriptures above and praying?

Now Go Pray

Find a place to pray. Take 5-10 minutes to pray the Lord's Prayer, 5-10 minutes about faith, and the rest about things important to you.

Prayer Journal

Use the Journal to record your experiences during prayer. You may want to record any thoughts that come into your mind or if you feel the Holy Spirit speaking to you.

DAY 2 - EVENING DEVOTION

Faith in Prayer

"Jesus answered them, "I tell you with certainty, if you have faith and do not doubt, not only will you be able to do what has been done to the fig tree, but you will also say to this mountain, 'Be removed and thrown into the sea,' and it will happen. You will receive whatever you ask for in prayer, if you believe"' Matthew 21:21-22 ISV

"But he must ask in faith, without any doubts, for the one who has doubts is like a wave of the sea that is driven and tossed by the wind. Such a person should not expect to receive anything from the Lord." James 1:6-7 ISV

Webster's Dictionary defines faith this way: "Belief; the assent of the mind to the truth of what is declared by another, resting on his authority and veracity, without other evidence; the judgment that what another states or testifies is the truth." Today, let's eliminate doubt and get our mind to believe what our heart has asked for. We will rest in the authority of God's promise to answer our prayer, however big or small. Without evidence, we choose to believe God will answer simply because we trust him. We are going to trust God because of the awesome truths about him in the Bible. We are going to trust God because of everything he has done for others and us in the past.

Let's Review

1. Do you have any doubt God will answer your prayer? If so, why?

2. What can you do to eliminate those doubts?

3. Try to find 2-3 scriptures about trusting God and recite them. Did doing this help increase your faith?

Now Go Pray

Find a place to pray. Take 5-10 minutes to pray the Lord's Prayer, 5-10 minutes about removing doubt, and the rest about things important to you.

Prayer Journal

Use the Journal to record your experiences during prayer. You may want to record any thoughts that come into your mind or if you feel the Holy Spirit speaking to you.

DAY 3 - MORNING DEVOTION

Understand God's Wants to Answer Your Prayer

"You have not chosen me, but I have chosen you. I have appointed you to go and produce fruit that will last, so that whatever you ask the Father in my name, he will give it to you. John 15:16 ISV

"So far you haven't asked for anything in my name. Keep asking and you will receive, so that your joy may be complete." John 16:24 ISV

God's wants to answer your prayer . . .

1. **So that you will produce fruit. (John 15:16)** Share what God has done in your life with others so they can receive his blessings as well and so God can receive the glory.

2. **He wants you to have complete joy. (John 16:24)** Just as earthly parents wants to make their children happy by giving them the things they need, so does our heavenly Father. It pleases him to see us happy and satisfied.

Pray with the understanding that God wants to give you the things you need so you can bless others and live in joy and happiness.

Let's Review

1. When God answers your specific prayer, what fruit will it produce and how will you be able to bless others? How will God be glorified?

2. List specific ways you believe your joy increase when God answers your prayer.

Now Go Pray

Find a place to pray. Take 5-10 minutes to pray the Lord's Prayer, 5-10 minutes about how you and others will be blessed when you receive the answer to your prayer, and the rest about things important to you.

Prayer Journal

Use the Journal to record your experiences during prayer. You may want to record any thoughts that come into your mind or if you feel the Holy Spirit speaking to you.

DAY 3 - EVENING DEVOTION

Asking in God's Will

"And this is the confidence that we have in him: if we ask for anything according to his will, he listens to us. And if we know that he listens to our requests, we can be sure that we have what we ask him for." 1 John 5:14-15 ISV

The things we ask for should be based on God's will, which is his purpose and plan for our life. This means we ask for the things we know he wants us to have. When we ask in God's will, we have confidence that he hears and will answer us. Having faith to wait on God and knowing that he will answer us when we have confidently asked for what is in his will.

Ask God if what you have been praying for is in his will. If so, have confidence he will answer you. If what you have been praying for is not in God, then ask him to show you what you should be praying for.

Let's Review

1. Have you asked God to show you if what you are praying for is in his will?

    Yes ___ No ___

2. If what you have been praying for is in God's will, what do you plan to do? If not, what will you do?

Now Go Pray

Find a place to pray. Take 5-10 minutes to pray the Lord's Prayer. Take 5-10 minutes and seriously pray about the will of God for your life and try to determine whether you are asking for is the same as what God has planned for you. Look over the review questions while you are praying. Talk to God about what you wrote and other important things in your life.

Prayer Journal

Use the Journal to record your experiences during prayer. You may want to record any thoughts that come into your mind or if you feel the Holy Spirit speaking to you.

DEVOTIONAL PART 2

SEEKING GOD

DAY 4 - MORNING DEVOTION

Prepare Your Heart to Seek God

"For Ezra had prepared his heart to seek the law of the LORD, and to do it, and to teach in Israel statutes and judgments." Ezra 7:10 KJV

Ezra was successful in petitioning King Ataxerxes to allow his people to return home, gathering those who wanted to migrate back to Jerusalem, and rebuilding the Jewish temple because he prepared his heart to seek God. Preparing your heart to seek God involve planning and thinking about what you need to seek God. You should take time to plan how much prayer, fasting, Bible study, and any other research needed, then task you wish to accomplish and your prayer will be answered. Write what you want in prayer and create a plan of how to get it.

Time for Action

1. Fill out your How to Ask, Seek & Knock in Prayer Goal Sheet available on my website.

If you cannot access it, then fill out the following:

A. I want God to . . .

B. To get what I am asking for, I am going to pray ___ hour(s) each day, ___ day(s) each week at ___AM/PM.

C. To get what I am asking for, I am going to read ___ chapter(s) in my Bible each day for ___ week(s) at ___ AM/PM.

D. To get what I am asking for, I am going to fast ___ day(s) each week for ___ week(s).

E. List anything you feel may be necessary to achieve your spiritual goal.

    1.

    2.

    3.

    4.

Now Go Pray

Find a place to pray. Take 5-10 minutes to review and pray about the commitment you just made. Next, take 5-10 minutes to pray the Lord's Prayer and the rest of the important things in your life.

Prayer Journal

Use the Journal to record your experiences during prayer. You may want to record any thoughts that come into your mind or if you feel the Holy Spirit speaking to you.

DAY 4 - EVENING DEVOTION

Seeking God Early

"I love them that love me; and those that seek me early shall find me." Proverbs 8:17 KJV

The best time to seek God is early in the morning while we are fresh, uninterrupted and before our complicated schedule gets in the way. When you get serious about seeking God, you will make him a priority in your life. Schedule time, perhaps even set your alarm to wake early tomorrow to seek God and pray.

Time for Action

1. Do you think there is a difference between praying early in the morning and at other times? Why or why not?

2. Can you think of anyone in the Bible who got up early to pray? What difference do you think this made in their lives?

Now Go Pray

Find a place to pray. Take 5 minutes to read and review the scriptures above. Pray about your plan to seek God early tomorrow, in addition praying about the topics in the Lord's Prayer and the rest of the important things in your life.

Prayer Journal

Use the Journal to record your experiences during prayer. You may want to record any thoughts that come into your mind or if you feel the Holy Spirit speaking to you.

DAY 5 - MORNING DEVOTION

Seeking God Early

"A Psalm of David, when he was in the wilderness of Judah. O God, thou art my God; early will I seek thee: my soul thirsteth for thee, my flesh longeth for thee in a dry and thirsty land, where no water is; To see thy power and thy glory, so as I have seen thee in the sanctuary." Psalms 63:1-2 KJV

Some people have a deep, passionate desire to know God and do his will while others do not. David's desire to seek God was great and drove him to seek God early. To him, the need to pray was similar to a hungry person craving food or a thirsty person desiring water. He hungered and thirsted after God. Jesus said:

> *"Blessed are they which do hunger and thirst after righteousness: for they shall be filled."* Matthew 5:6 KJV

Those who have a deep passion for God are blessed. Pray about your passion to seek God.

Questions for Reflection

1. During the time spent undertaking this devotional, have you become more passionate about seeking God? Why or why not?

2. Does praying early in the morning feel different from praying at other times of the day? If so, how?

Now Go Pray

Find a place to pray. Take 5 minutes to review the scripture above and think about what it means to hunger and thirst for god. Pray about what it takes to have passion for God, in addition praying about the topics in the Lord's Prayer, seeking God early, and the rest of the important things in your life.

Challenge Yourself

Instead of trying to find time for prayer and seeking God, make time. Download the free *How to Ask, Seek and Knock Prayer Calendar* on my website. If you cannot access or locate the calendar, create a prayer weekly or monthly calendar. Schedule time for prayer each week and keep track of your results.

Prayer Journal

Use the Journal to record your experiences during prayer. You may want to record any thoughts that come into your mind or if you feel the Holy Spirit speaking to you.

DAY 5 - EVENING DEVOTION

Seek God with all Your Heart, Mind, and Strength

"Everything that Hezekiah began in the service of God's Temple was done according to the Law and to the commandments as he sought his God, worked with all of his heart, and became successful." 2 Chronicles 31:21 ISV

God will give us success when we seek him with all our heart. We need to show him how serious we are by putting our best effort into seeking him and to get our prayers answered. Remember, receiving the answer to our prayer can potentially change our life or someone else. With so much at stake, can we afford to seek God half-heartedly?

Time for Action

1. In the past, can you say that you prayed and sought god with all your heart? Why or why not?

2. What do you think you need to do to seek God with all your heart? What effect do you think this will have on your prayer life and walk with God

Now Go Pray

Find a place to pray. Take 5 minutes to review the scripture above and think about what it takes to give God all your heart. Pray about seeking God with all your heart, in addition praying about the topics in the Lord's Prayer and the rest of the important things in your life.

Prayer Journal

Use the Journal to record your experiences during prayer. You may want to record any thoughts that

come into your mind or if you feel the Holy Spirit speaking to you.

DEVOTIONAL PART 3

KNOCKING

DAY 6 - MORNING DEVOTION

Have a Sense of Urgency

"Seek the LORD while he may be found, call upon him while he is near." Isaiah 55:6 ISV

We need to seek God while we have the opportunity. Whether know the Lord calling us to seek him or we feel an unknown desire to draw closer, now is the time to do all we can to deepen our spiritual walk. The Bible tells us there are times when God moves closer to us than other times. In those times, he is trying to draw closer to us. Consider John 6:44:

> *"No one can come to me unless the Father who sent me draws him, and I will raise him to life on the last day."* John 6:44 ISV

While God is drawing you closer, draw closer to him, with the goal of discovering what he wants to do in your life.

Time for Action

1. Do you feel God drawing you closer to him or did you make a decision to be closer to God without him calling you? Why do you think so?

2. Why do you think it is important to seek God while he is close to you?

Now Go Pray

Find a place to pray. Take 5-10 minutes to review the scriptures above and your answers. Think about why it is important to seek God while he is close to you. Pray about what you have done so far and how it has affected your spiritual journey. Don't forget to pray about the topics in the Lord's

Prayer and the rest of the important things in your life.

Prayer Journal

Use the Journal to record your experiences during prayer. You may want to record any thoughts that come into your mind or if you feel the Holy Spirit speaking to you.

DAY 6 - EVENING DEVOTION

Search Yourself

So far, you have been asked to pray the Lord's Prayer, make plans, and seek God early in prayer. This goes a long way toward seeking God with all your heart, mind, and strength. Today, think about everything you have been doing so far and the effect it has had on your efforts of Asking and Seeking God.

Time for Action

1. What effect have the past five days had on your spiritual walk?

2. Is there anything else you feel that you could do to ensure you will be successful in seeking God? Think about things friends,

family, coworkers, or people in the Bible have done to have major prayers in their lives answered and record them.

Now Go Pray

Find a place to pray. Take 5 minutes to review your answers and think about what it takes to give God all your heart. Pray about what you have done so far and how it has affected your spiritual journey. Don't forget to pray about the topics in the Lord's Prayer and the rest of the important things in your life.

Prayer Journal

Use the Journal to record your experiences during prayer. You may want to record any thoughts that

come into your mind or if you feel the Holy Spirit speaking to you.

DAY 7 - MORNING DEVOTION

Overcoming Obstacles

"'I know what you've been doing. Look! I have put in front of you an open door that no one can shut. You have only a little strength, but you have obeyed my word and have not denied my name." Revelation 3:8 ISV

Jesus said in Matthew 7:7 if we knocked, he would open the door. If we are seeking God and praying, one would think the door would be opened by the end of our journey. Closed doors symbolize final obstacles that obstruct us from receiving answers to our prayers. If we want our prayers answered 100% percent of the time, then we have to learn how to open closed doors.

Jesus told the church of Philadelphia in Revelation 3:8 that he opened the door for them and no one would be able to shut it. Why was their door open? Two reasons: They obeyed God's word and did not deny the name of Jesus. When we obey God's word and hold fast to the name of Jesus in difficult circumstances, doors will open for u. Pray for Jesus to open any doors that may be standing in your way.

Time for Action

1. Are there any obstacles (or doors) that you feel are obstructing your prayers from being answered? If so, list them.

2. What do you think you could do to overcome any obstacles obstructing your prayers?

Now Go Pray

Find a place to pray. Take 5 minutes to review your answers. Think about how close you are to receiving the answer to your prayer and any obstacle that may be in the way. Pray about what it may take to overcome any obstacles. Don't forget to pray about the topics in the Lord's Prayer and the rest of the important things in your life.

Prayer Journal

Use the Journal to record your experiences during prayer. You may want to record any thoughts that come into your mind or if you feel the Holy Spirit speaking to you.

DAY 7 - EVENING DEVOTION

Determination

"He said, "In a city there was a judge who didn't fear God or respect people. In that city there was also a widow who kept coming to him and saying, 'Grant me justice against my adversary.' For a while the judge refused. But later he told himself, 'I don't fear God or respect people, yet because this widow keeps bothering me, I will grant her justice. Otherwise, she will keep coming and wear me out.'" Then the Lord added, "Listen to what the unrighteous judge says. Won't God grant his chosen people justice when they cry out to him day and night? Is he slow to help them? I tell you, he will give them justice quickly. But when the Son of Man comes, will he find faith on earth?" Luke 18:2-8 ISV

Knocking represents determination. It shows our determination to continue calling on God, even if it seems as if he is not answering. Jesus encourages us to continue seeking God, night and day, if we are serious about what we want. Sometimes it seems as if we are at the end of our spiritual journey and ready to receive what we asked God for, but adversity or setbacks dampen our hope. We expect our prayers to be answered, but rarely do we expect adversity. We have to develop the strength and perseverance to wait patiently until Jesus opens the door. Remember the journey has been too long to give at the door. Pray for the determination to continue asking, seeking, and knocking, although circumstances make it seem like your prayer is not being answered.

Time for Action

1. 1 Samuel 30:1-26 says that David had a major setback, but encouraged himself. In the end, he gained more than he lost. Read these verses and list the ways that you can encourage yourself.

Now Go Pray

Find a place to pray. Take 5 minutes to review your answers. Think about ways to encourage yourself when you have a setback. Have you or do you know anyone who had a setback that turned into a great blessing? Think about that situation and pray about what it may take to overcome any obstacles. Don't forget to pray about the topics in the Lord's Prayer and the rest of the important things in your life.

Prayer Journal

Use the Journal to record your experiences during prayer. You may want to record any thoughts that come into your mind or if you feel the Holy Spirit speaking to you.

AUTHOR BIOGRAPHY

Benjamin Reynolds is an author and ordained minister. He earned a Bachelor of Arts degree in Law and Society from Michigan State University and has a Masters of Christian Studies degree from Master's International School of Divinity. He later earned a Certificate Diploma in Client Server programming and worked for more than ten years as a computer programmer. An avid reader and student of Bible prophecy, Christian literature has always been a fascination of his. He wrote his first novel, When the Trumpet Sounds, Examining the Resurrection of the Church, in 2007 after complications with Ulcerative Colitis, resulted in a near death experience. Benjamin felt a deep desire to research, deepen his understanding and knowledge of Bible Prophecy, the afterlife, prayer, fasting, miracles, healing, angels and demons.

Benjamin credits his faith, positive outlook, friends and family with helping him successfully endure and recuperate from four major surgeries in 2006 to 2008, as well as being able to overcome continuing health challenges. The author of nine books, he is passionate about writing in the Christian fiction and non-fiction genres. Benjamin also serves as a Senior Pastor, as Foreign Missions Secretary for the Metropolitan Apostolic Fellowship organization and regularly ministers to churches in the United States, Canada and the Philippines.

Questions for the Author?

Email me at info@benjaminlreynolds.com or visit
www.benjaminlreynolds.com

MORE FROM BENJAMIN L. REYNOLDS

Ask and It Shall Be Given: 3 Steps to Guaranteed Results in Prayer

Jesus promised that everyone who asked in prayer would receive. With such an incredible guarantee, why are we not receiving everything we ask for? Either Matthew 7:7-8 is not true, or we need to learn the true meaning of *Asking, Seeking and Knocking*. It's time to take hold of the promise and begin *Asking, Seeking and Knocking* our way toward **guaranteed** results!

http://www.amazon.com/dp/B00BD4YOKY

The Ten Greatest Prayers of the Bible

This thorough study of the Bible's greatest prayers reveals astounding truths about prayer and how to achieve miraculous results. Featuring actual prayers from biblical heroes such as Solomon, Hezekiah, Jesus and many others, this book shows you how to pray and achieve results from God the way that spiritual giants of the Bible did.

http://www.amazon.com/dp/B0057YJIHU

The Ten Greatest Miracles of the Bible

The Bible contains over 114 miracles in 6 categories, including the human body, nature, military intervention, food, animals, and finances. It examines the Bibles' greatest miracles and describes the steps to experiencing great miracles in your life. The Ten Greatest Miracles of the Bible is a thorough study of the Bible's greatest miracles and reveals astounding truths about nature of miracles and how they are manifested. Prepare to experience the divine power of God and experience miracles the way great people of the Bible did.

http://www.amazon.com/dp/B008EPLTGM

The Ten Greatest Prayers and Miracles of the Bible Combo Pack

Two Books for one! This book contains both The Ten Greatest Prayers of the Bible and The Ten Greatest Miracles of the Bible.

http://www.amazon.com/dp/B008IAEM9Y

40 Days of Faith

40 Days of Faith is a devotional designed to bring individuals closer to Christ by following the examples of people in the Bible such as Moses and Jesus Christ who spent 40 days with the Lord. Your life will be changed through 40 days of reading a Bible verses each day, prayer, fasting and seeking the Lord. Prepare to become spiritually stronger and anointed through this book!

http://www.amazon.com/dp/B005G69H9S

Ready for the Rapture

Examine the definition of the resurrection, the signs of the Second Coming of Jesus Christ, the relationship between the Tribulation Period and the

Second Coming of Jesus Christ, if the resurrection is different from the Second Coming of Jesus Christ, an examination of "The Resurrection Parables", and the current state of the Church. Includes 31 scriptures and a 20-item checklist to see if you are ready for the rapture!

http://www.amazon.com/dp/B006ECW92A

Living in the New Millennium and Beyond

Have you ever wondered about life after Jesus Christ returns to the earth, the Day of Judgment, the New Heaven and the New Earth and the rewards of the saints? With over 125 referenced scriptures, this book answers those questions.

http://www.amazon.com/dp/B004QGYDAW

Ready for the Rapture and Living in the New Millennium and Beyond Combo Pack

Two Books for one! This book contains both Ready for the Rapture and Living in the New Millennium and Beyond books in one.

http://www.amazon.com/dp/B008I5FFK4

Seven Years Until Eternity: The Rise of the Antichrist

The antichrist rises to power using satanic forces, world leaders, one world religion, and currency to control the entire earth. The struggle of humanity, angels, and demons rages across earth to the gates of heaven with the final victory being determined at the battle of Armageddon!

http://www.amazon.com/dp/B0045OULO2

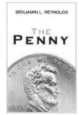

The Penny

Randal Cole is the beleaguered pastor of a small, inner city storefront church. On the day he decides to resign, Randal is approached by mysterious man outside of his church and asked to do something very strange...place a penny in the offering plate the coming Sunday. Randal agrees, and quickly finds out that he is not the only one that this man has approached with this unusual request. He soon finds himself at the center of a global movement that radically transforms him, his church, and people throughout the world like never before.

Who was this strange man? Why was Randal and his small, seemingly insignificant church chosen?

http://www.amazon.com/dp/B007BTQTYY

5/14

29567956R00094

Made in the USA
Charleston, SC
16 May 2014